Dialogue and Interfaith Witness with MUSLIMS

A Guide and Sample Ministry in the U.S.A.

by Ray G. Register, Jr.

DIALOGUE AND INTERFAITH WITNESS WITH MUSLIMS

All Scripture quotations are from the *Revised Standard Version* of the Bible © 1946, 1952, 1971, 1973. All Quotations from the *Quran* are the author's interpretation from the Arabic.

First Edition

Library of Congress Catalog No.: 79-6575
ISBN: 0-9603018-0-1

Distributed in the U.S.A.
by
MOODY BOOKS INC.
469 E. Sullivan St.
Kingsport, TN 37660
(615) 246-6452

PRINTED IN THE UNITED STATES OF AMERICA
by
WATSON LITHOGRAPHING COMPANY
P.O.B. 537 Kingsport, TN 37662

Cover designed by Peggy Hartsock
Cover photo: Modern Nazareth; the Mosque of Peace and the Basilica of the Annunciation, taken by the author.

CONTENTS

A PERSONAL MESSAGE

by

Dr. George W. Braswell, Jr.

Ray Register has immersed himself in Arab-Muslim culture for over a decade, mastering the Arabic language, penetrating the symbols and meanings of Islam, and initiating a communication process between Christians and Muslims which has had deep impact in his work with the peoples of the Galilee.

This book provides a larger audience the opportunity to understand the religion, Islam, to visualize Muslims who practice Islam, and to encounter a way to communicate meaning fully with Muslims. Insights into the theology, ethics, scriptures, and religious behavior of Muslims are excellent. Communication methods based on integrity of and appreciation for Muslims are clearly presented. And the Christian principles of theology and ethics are constantly applied to the encounters between Christians and Muslims.

Wherever one may have opportunity to speak with Muslims, this book offers a concise and pointed help. It not only gives one a handle for beginning a meaningful conversation with a Muslim, but it also takes one into the depths of understanding the process of communication between a Christian and a Muslim.

George W. Braswell, Jr.
Professor of Missions and World Religions
Southeastern Baptist Theological Seminary
Wake Forest, North Carolina

PREFACE

An age of growing Arab and Muslim influence in the fields of economics, politics and religion is upon us. Many books have been written to inform the English speaking people about Islam, the religion of nearly 720 million Muslims. However, the Christian who is committed to sharing the Gospel with Muslims in an intelligent way finds little to guide him. He soon discovers that neither he nor his Muslim friend understands each other. The Christian finds the meaning of his words distorted. An argument breaks out. Friendship is broken. He is left feeling that he has said and done the wrong thing. This is as true of the missionary in a Muslim country as it is for the Christian who wants to befriend a Muslim international in Europe or America.

The following "Guide to Dialogue and Interfaith Witness with Muslims" is an attempt to understand and to overcome the difficulties that block communication with Muslims. Chapter I contains a brief history of Islam with a short description of the life of Muhammad and his teachings. This is to be considered a minimum coverage and should be supplemented by further study. In Chapter II "Dialogue as a Method of Approach to Muslims" will be discussed in its theological and historical perspective. The barriers to the Christian-Muslim dialogue will be clarified. Chapter III offers some general guidelines for sharing your faith. It challenges you to dialogue, rather than to monologue. Christian dialogue has as its ideal the Incarnation of God in Christ Jesus of Nazareth. In Christ, God initiated a personal dialogue to reconcile sinful man to himself (II Corinthians 5:17-19). Dialogue assumes that we are as willing to learn what the Muslim thinks as we are to share our faith with him. In dialogue both Christian and Muslim grow together in understanding, rather than telling each other what to believe. Each bears witness to his faith, while at the same time facing squarely the differences that divide the two faiths.

The general objectives which underlie the approach of this Guide to Dialogue and Interfaith Witness with Muslims are two-fold:

First; You are encouraged to get to know the Muslim as a person. This means forming a genuine friendship with him and sharing his personal concerns. In the process, the Muslim comes to know you as a person who shares the concerns of a common humanity of which he is a special part. His religion is an integral part of his life. Therefore, you will learn as much as possible about what he believes about God.

Second; You are challenged to share your faith in Christ with the Muslim. This sharing should develop naturally from your personal relationship with the Muslim. Your faith will be challenged and redefined as you attempt to communicate with the Muslim. His understanding of God will be affected as your life-style and words exhibit the love that Christ alone inspires.

Chapter IV deals with some typical questions and statements that a Muslim will use when discussing his religion with a Christian. Keep in mind that the Muslim learns these questions in school as a child. He assumes that Islam is the true faith and that Christianity has been perverted. He already knows the usual answers that Christians give to these questions and is ready with rebuttals, which usually result in debate, argument, and a monologue. If you refuse to answer, he will simply think that he is right in his assumptions. His questions can however be used as a natural point of departure for dialogue, if we understand the underlying thoughts and feelings behind them. The "Guide" offers ideas for answers which will stimulate discussion and will be in keeping with his thought forms. Dialogue, or true communication, will follow.

The "Scripture to Scripture" approach is used to lead from the Muslim's question to a study of what the Bible says on the subject. Although the Muslim believes that the Qur'an is the literal word of God in Arabic, he may also hold a high regard for the Bible, particularly if he has attended a mission school. He does believe that Christians and Jews have perverted its meaning. Therefore, the appeal of the "Guide" is not to man's opinions, or traditions, but to what God has said through Holy Scripture. He will respect your knowledge of the Bible, especially if it clarifies issues that have divided Christians and Muslims for centuries.

Chapter V is a summary of guidelines for dialogue. These will be practical suggestions to prepare you for conversation and interfaith witness with Muslims.

Chapter VI will offer suggestions on what to do for a person who decides to change his or her faith either as a result of dialogue or for other reasons. The first part will deal with the attitude toward a person who has been a Christian, but decides to convert to Islam. The second part will offer guidelines for encouraging a Muslim who decides to follow Christ.

Many of the insights shared in this "Guide" were gained as a result of my twelve years of experience living and working with the Arab minority in Israel as a representative of the Southern Baptist Foreign Mission Board. These Arabs have been separated from the mainstream of Islam since 1948. Many lack the intellectual sophistication of Muslims you may meet in Beirut, Cairo, or Tehran. Most have been Sunni Muslims. I have had only limited acquaintances with the Shi'ite Muslims of Persia or Iran and Lebanon. Bearing these limitations in mind, you will want to supplement the "Guide" with a personal study of Islam and the Muslims of your area. An extensive bibliography is included at the end to assist you. **The Arab World Today,** by Morroe Berger, is recommended as an introduction to the Muslim life-style.

Appendix I provides a sample ministry to Muslims in the U.S.A. which illustrates a possible project of interfaith witness with Muslims.

Several books have provided confirmation of my views on dialogue with Muslims. **The Miracle of Dialogue,** by Reuel L. Howe, has provided valuable insights into the ministry of dialogue. The "Scripture to Scripture" approach is encouraged by Geoffrey Parrinder in **Jesus in the Quran**. An excellent historical and philosophical study by Dr. Akbar Abdul-Haqq is found in his **Christ in the New Testament and the Quran**. The recently published proceedings of the North American Conference on Muslim Evangelization **The Gospel and Islam, a 1978**

Compendium is especially relevant. Helpful material has been received through the "Fellowship of Faith for the Muslims" (FFM) in Toronto, Ontario, Canada.

Quotations from the Quran are my personal translation from the Arabic text, using the Egyptian numeration of verses found in **The Holy Quran**, by A. Yusif Ali which may differ by one or more verses from other translations. Some translators count the Arabic blessing, **Bismallah** (In the name of God), as a verse and others do not. A chapter of the Quran is called a **Surah** in Arabic. Each **Surah** bears a title taken from a significant word in that chapter of the Quran. These titles are given in both English and Arabic transliteration for ease in using them with the Muslim. Key Arabic phrases are transliterated into English and placed in parenthesis to assist the reader. **Surah** numbers appear in Roman numerals. Arabic romanization, or transliteration, is that which has been approved by the American Library Association and the Library of Congress Cataloging Service and is published in Bulletin 91 of September 1970. For ease in reading, the following words are written in their popular form because of their frequent usage:

> **Qur'an** is written as "Quran," **Muhammad** as "Muhammad," **Khalifa** as "Caliph," **Surah** as "Surah," **Shi^{c}ite** as "Shi'ite," and **Ka^{c}bah** as "Ka'bah."

This Guide has been written, tested, and revised as a project in ministry for the Doctor of Ministry Degree at the Southeastern Baptist Theological Seminary at Wake Forest, North Carolina. I am grateful to members of the faculty, friends, and representatives of the Southern Baptist Home and Foreign Mission Boards who have helped with the revision. I owe a special debt of gratitude to Dr. Roland E. Miller of Luther College, Saskatchewan, Canada for corrections to the final published text.

The Guide is dedicated to all the "Sons of Ishmael" and to those who strive to share the glory of God revealed in Christ with them.

INTRODUCTION

The Muslim, by definition, is a person who is "surrendered" or "submitted" to the will of God, and is a follower of Islam, the religion of the Arab Prophet Muhammad (c. 570-632 A.D.)[1] A majority of the Arab people are Muslim by religion. Only ten percent are Christians.[2] Whether he be an Arab, a Persian, a Pakistani, an Indonesian, an African, or a Turk, the Muslim is a person who is committed to God according to the best spiritual knowledge that he has. Islam is precious to him as his religion, his culture, and his very life. Unfortunately, Islam represents a distorted and negative view of Christianity which makes the average Muslim very resistant to the Gospel as we understand it. The rejection of Jesus' death on the cross is the major barrier to the Muslim understanding of the Christian faith. The purpose of this "Guide" is to assist you in overcoming this barrier through dialogue and interfaith witness.

Dialogue is an attempt to bridge the "communication gap" that has existed between Christians and Muslims for centuries. Dialogue permits the Christian and the Muslim to share their faith in God with each other on the deepest levels of personal experience. For the committed Christian and the dedicated Muslim, dialogue leads inevitably to interfaith witness as friendship deepens. This has both its rewards and its dangers, as will be seen.

The basic motivation of dialogue, for the Christian, is the Incarnation of God in Jesus Christ through the Holy Spirit for the reconciliation of sinful man to himself. God came in Christ to reconcile man to himself and to other men through the cross. The Christian is called to be a messenger of this reconciliation to other persons (II Corinthians 5: 17-19). Dialogue is a means of bringing reconciliation between Christian and Muslim through a sharing of friendship and God's revelation.

This reconciliation has been called the "miracle of dialogue" by Reuel Howe in his book by that name:

> If Christians would be like Christ, they must expect to become dialogical persons to and through whom he may speak . . . The dialogical role is often misinterpreted to mean that one does not take a stand . . . On the contrary, the dialogical role is to take a stand.[3]

Dialogue with Muslims is not for the weak in faith. It is for those who are committed to sharing their faith in Christ even though there are risks involved in being open to another's faith. It is a sharing and not a monologue. The Muslim will expect you to tell him about Christ. If you do not, he will suspect your motivation, especially if you are a representative of your church. In the process he deserves "equal time" and your wholehearted understanding.

When a Christian and a Muslim enter into dialogue about spiritual matters, it may be discovered that the Muslim is just as committed to sharing his faith as is the Christian. Islam, like Christianity, is a growing missionary faith. Both must bear witness to their faith. Islam is competing with Christianity for the hearts of Black Africans. Islamic centers can be found in Europe and the United States. The attitude of Muslims toward Christians has been formed in the heat of intense religious and political rivalry since Islam's beginning in the seventh century after Christ. The past record of Christian-Muslim interchange could be called a two-sided monologue. Christians attacked Muslims for their refusal to accept Jesus as the Son of God. Muslims charged Christians with **shirk**, or polytheism, because of the Christian belief in the Trinity. The world is too small for this controversy to continue. In the following pages let us try to hear the Muslim and to share our faith in a way that he might understand.

I
A BRIEF HISTORY OF ISLAM

Islam is the faith of over 720 million people in the world today.[1] It is second only to Christianity as the world's largest monotheistic religion. Islam, more than merely a religion, is a culture that in its glory led the world in philosophy, science, and medicine while the western world lay in the "Dark Ages." Over two million Muslim people are estimated to live in the United States today, including students and permanent residents. Other millions live in Europe. This offers an unusual opportunity for dialogue and interfaith witness with Christians.

Islam dates its beginning from the year 622 A.D., the year of the **Hijrah**, when the Arab Prophet Muhammad "migrated" or fled from persecution in Mecca to the city of Yathrib, which was later renamed al-Medina, the city of the Prophet. Muhammad was born about 570 A.D. into the ruling Quraish tribe of Mecca in Arabia. His father died before his birth and his mother shortly thereafter. He was raised as an orphan by relatives. The Quraish controlled the commercial, political, and religious life of the pagan Arab tribes that came yearly to worship in Mecca at the Ka'bah, the shrine of a black stone which was believed to have fallen from heaven. Muhammad was a deeply sensitive, spiritual inquirer, who at the age of forty claimed to receive revelations from God. He was then married to Khadija, a wealthy widow, for whom he worked as a caravan leader. She became his first convert as he preached against paganism, the exploitation of the Quraish, and the theological confusion in the Christian and Jewish communities of Arabia. He and his followers were persecuted by the Quraish to such an extent that they fled to Medina in 622 A.D. There, with the support of relatives loyal to him, he set up a religious and political theocracy that was to become the model for later

Islamic states. In 630 A.D. he returned to Mecca as a conqueror, cleansed the sacred precincts of the Ka'bah of pagan idols, and united the warring pagan Arab tribes in allegiance to him and to the one true God, Allah.[2] He died only two years later at the age of sixty-two. Abu Bakr, his first male convert, became his successor or "Caliph."

The relevations to Muhammad, recorded by his followers in the Quran, repeated much of what was taught by Judaism, but with a distinctly Arabic flavor. He claimed Abraham as the father of Muslims. Ishmael, Abraham's son by the slave Hagar, was the forefather of the Arabs. Reverence for all the prophets, especially Adam, Abraham, Noah, Moses, and Jesus was taught. Muhammad, according to the Quran, was the final "Seal of the Prophets" (XXXIII:40) and his revelations were inclusive of all that came before him.

Orthodox Islam requires of its followers the simple confession of faith in one God, Allah, and in Muhammad as his prophet. Devout Muslims pray five times daily, facing Mecca. They fast one month a year during the Month of Ramadan, which by tradition was the month the Quran was revealed to Muhammad. They give 2-1/2% of their income to the poor, and perform the **hajj**, or pilgrimage to Mecca once in a lifetime. These basic requirements are called the "Five Pillars of Islam" (al-awamid al-khamisa).

Muslims regard Islam as a social as well as a religious reform movement. Muhammad forbade the pagan practice of killing unwanted baby girls. A woman could inherit one-half the value of a man's inheritance. A man was permitted to marry four wives; but he must be able to provide for each equally. Compared to former pagan practice Muhammad elevated the status of women. He commanded the compassionate treatment of orphans. After the death of Khadija he had eleven wives partly as a result of political alliances, and what he claimed as special dispensation from God (XXXIII:50-52). The trend in most Muslim countries today is toward monogamy.

The Quran is the collection of Muhammad's revelations which he claimed to receive from God through the angel Gabriel. Written in Arabic of the Meccan dialect, it has a unique quality that fascinates the listener. The language of the Quran has set the standard for the classical Arabic language. The Quran is considered Muhammad's one miracle. Its major theme is the justice of God and a warning of Hellfire for all unbelievers. About one-third of the Quran is a repetition of Bible stories but with changes in content and style. The source of differences between the Quran and the Bible can usually be found in Jewish traditions and the Apocryphal Gospels, particularly those held to be heretical by the Church councils.

A popular tradition with both Muslim and Christian Arabs is that Muhammad received both confirmation and material for his revelations from a heretical priest named Sergius, or "Bahira."[3] Nevertheless, devout Muslims will deny the possibility that Muhammad received any knowledge from Bahira since they believed his revelations came directly from God through the angel Gabriel.

Islam eventually divided into two major groups following the death of Muhammad in 632 A.D. The majority followed the Caliphs who rose to authority, beginning with Abu Bakr. They are called the "Sunnites." The title refers to the "practices" or "Sunna" of the Prophet Muhammad that became the pattern of life for orthodox Muslims. Four schools of law governing civil and religious life developed in Sunni Islam and are followed in various countries of the Middle East.[4]

The "Shi'ites," on the other hand, disagreed with the appointment of Abu Bakr as Caliph. They believed that Muhammad had appointed his own son-in-law, Ali, as his rightful successor. "Shi'ah" is the Arabic word for a "party" or "faction." It can also mean "practice."

The Shi'ites believe that there were rightful successors or "Imams" to Muhammad. They are divided into sects which disagree on the number of the Imams. The last of the Imams disappeared and is called the "Mehdi." The Mehdi, or rightly guided Imam, will reappear someday and restore true Islam, according to Shi'ite belief. The majority of Muslims in Iran are Shi'ites.[5]

Muhammad's followers carried Islam as a religious, political, and military movement from China to the Atlantic Ocean by 715 A.D. The rapid Arab expansion can be attributed partly to the vigor of the new faith of Islam and partly to the degeneration of the Christian Byzantine empire that had heavily taxed the subjects of its area. Islam adopted the cultures and intellectual sophistication of the people it subjected. It preserved vast areas of knowledge in the fields of medicine, astronomy, and mathematics while Europe was in its "Dark Ages." The surge of Arab influence in today's world is in part due to the dream of returning to the past glory of Islam.

The mindset of the Arab Muslim has been molded by his past. He is a strong individualist and a natural born leader, which often sets him at odds with his peers. At the same time he is under strong social pressure to remain loyal to his family and tribe. Any breach of this loyalty can result in great shame being heaped upon him. He seldom accepts blame and is deeply suspicious of other Arabs. He is given to displays of generous hospitality and readily accepts strangers who show interest in his Islamic culture and the Arabic language. He is capable of lasting friendhship but can heap bitter verbal condemnation upon any enemy. His volatile and sensitive nature is tempered in social relations by a strong code of respect (karamah) and the use of an intermediary (wastah) to settle disputes. His major concerns are the breakdown of family life in the midst of increasing materialism, godless communism, and the humiliation of the Israeli-Palestinian conflict. The Christian who befriends a Muslim will be expected to be sensitive to his mindset and concerns.

II
DIALOGUE AS A METHOD OF APPROACH TO MUSLIMS

Dialogue has been defined by Reuel Howe as "the serious address and response between two or more persons, in which the being and truth of each is confronted by the being and truth of the other."[1] True dialogue employs both the language of relationship and the language of words. It seeks to know life through the other person. In dialogue, barriers to communication are broken down. Personhood is honored, and community is formed.[2]

Unfortunately, relationships between Christians and Muslims have all too often taken the form of heated monologue which creates defensiveness. Resort to monologue reveals a basic self-centeredness.

Dialogue, on the other hand, is motivated by outgoing love that seeks reconciliation through overcoming barriers to relationship. Reconciliation with Muslims is the theme of this chapter and the ultimate goal to which this Guide is dedicated.

Theological Basis of Dialogue: Incarnation

The doctrine of God and the doctrine of man are the central issues in the Christian-Muslim dialogue. The New Testament reveals that God desires to be reconciled to man who is estranged from him because of sin. Man is unable to save himself, or to change his inner rebellious nature. God, through Jesus Christ, became flesh (John 1:14), took the form of man in humility (Philippians 2:6-8), and died on the cross for man. In his death, Christ broke down the barrier between man and God, and man and his enemy, making peace (Ephesians 2:14). After his resurrection the Spirit was imparted, renewing man and empowering him for a ministry of reconciliation (II Corinthians 5:17-19). Howe notes that God himself initiated dialogue through the Incarnation:

> The Christian's hope is based on the belief that in Christ Jesus dialogue was revealed as a principle of renewal. His incarnation is understood to have been the occurrence of dialogue between man and man, in which God was fully participant; and, as we have seen, that which was begun in the incarnation of the Christ in Jesus is continued now through the incarnation of the Spirit in us.[3]

It was this understanding of God as a God of selfless love that attracted Dehqani-Tafti, a former Muslim, to Christianity:

> As I believe Christianity is the only religion that has shown God—who is a selfless god; who is a sacrificial god, a sacrificial love. And therefore I think the unique thing in Christianity (is) the incarnation and the cross, the crucifixion. Christianity believes in God who left his glory and came into the world . . . who left his palace and went to live with his subjects, as it were . . . Now, I don't know of any other religion that has this kind of concept of sacrificial love, of a God who gave up his own life for the sake of his enemies.[4]

This sacrificial, reconciling love of God revealed in the Incarnation provides the basic motivation for Christian-Muslim dialogue according to Paul Seto, veteran missionary to Muslims:

> But, to the question, what is the purpose of Christian-Muslim dialogue, what is the intention of Christian-Muslim relationships, I have a more basic answer. It is this, that obedience to the requirements of the Gospel, of our faith, demands that we be positively related to men of other faiths, in our case, the Muslims. We are commanded to love, as Christ loved us, to be reconcilers, even as in Christ we have been reconciled. In a profound way, the willingness and ability to deal respectfully, honestly, lovingly, patiently, hopefully, with those whom history, or circumstance, or our own misunderstandings have estranged from us, is a fruit of our faith and faithfulness.[5]

The basic motivation for dialogue, so eloquently stated by Dehqani-Tafti and Seto, unfortunately runs directly contrary to the Muslim understanding of God and man. Kenneth Cragg has faced squarely the conflict of the doctrine of the Incarnation with Islam:

> Islam claims that in its historic faith the Church has misconstrued the mission of Jesus. Since these "errors" involve the central points of the Christian understanding of Jesus, His Incarntaion, and His death upon the Cross, the issue admits to no reconciliation. The Muslim sees Islam correcting Christian "distortion" of Jesus and God. The Christian sees it disqualifying the heart of his understanding of both.[6]

The Incarnation is crucial because it is both the basic motivation as well as the content of dialogue. The Muslim denial of the Incarnation is a negation of the basis of the Christian life-style as well as the Christian understanding of God in Christ.

It would appear that the Muslim negation of the Incarnation makes dialogue an exercise in futility. However, the very estrangement caused by this negation can become a point of departure for dialogue. The burden is upon the Christian to initiate dialogue with Muslims, even on this controversial issue. If the Christian fails to deal with the issue of the Incarnation, experience has shown that the Muslim will challenge him to do so. Such is the experience of a former Jew who accepted Christ and began a ministry with Muslims in Iran:

> In our Muslim-Christian involvement we cannot bypass the controversial areas of the Sonship, the Lordship and the cross of Christ. It is precisely here that we should mostly be involved. One of our tasks is to rethink and recoin the traditional phrases so dearly cherished. The Sonship and the Lordship of Christ which are neither status or by adoption, as some of them think but relational and qualitative, should be seen in their relation to Christ's servanthood and Christ's obedience.[7]

The task of dialogue is not to avoid the basic issues but to face them, just as God in Christ faced our sinful state and won the victory by sacrificial love. A task of this book will be to "rethink and recoin the traditional phrases so dearly cherished" in order that the Muslim may share in their meaning.

Dialogue and Interfaith Witness

Dialogue in which the being and truth of each person is confronted by the being and truth of the other issues naturally in interfaith witness. In the Christian-Muslim context witness to one's faith is inevitable if either is committed to his faith. Both Christianity and Islam are missionary faiths. Each seeks to bring the entire world to God. To fail to deal with the theological issues involved is to fail to be true to that which is most meaningful to each participant in dialogue.

One's concept of dialogue determines his reaction to employing the term "witness" in the dialogical context. There is a limited concept which would maintain that witness is outside the scope of dialogue. This concept views dialogue as the dispassionate exchange of views for the sake of coming to some form of agreement. Persuasion with a view to convert a party in the dialogue is considered dishonest. Lying behind this view of dialogue is a basic objection to the monological approach which is characteristic of "soul-winning" and "plan of salvation" witnessing. Dialogue, according to this view, should not be used as a trap for unsuspecting individuals.

The honesty of the above objection to the use of witness in dialogue is granted, if one subscribes to a limited view of dialogue. However, in the Christian-Muslim context, this view borders on naiveté. No such dispassionate encounter between a Christian and Muslim can be expected, if either or both are committed to their faith. Dialogue which is grounded in the revelations of both faiths leads inevitably to interfaith witness which may issue in the persuasion of one or both to change his views. Both must take a stand, according to Howe:

> The dialogical role is often misinterpreted to mean that one does not take a stand, especially a stand against what seems to be a majority. On the contrary, the dialogical role means to take a stand.[8]

Dialogue, in its more inclusive sense, issues in change and renewal because both parties have been true to themselves. In taking a stand they have laid the foundation of honestly on which reconciliation can be built, if the truth is spoken in love.

Another limited view of dialogue sees it as an attempt to syncretise the two religions. Some evangelicals would object to the use of the term "dialogue" because they fear it would compromise the uniqueness of Christianity. Dehqani-Tafti emphasises that dialogue is not syncretism:

> I think it is not syncretism; it's not merging either. I'm not proposing a federation of all religions. It is contact in the spirit of the cross, with the other man. The spirit of the cross is unique. The spirit of incarnation is unique. But one has to have contact with the other chap to interpret this for him in such a way that he may understand.[9]

Dialogue, for the Christian, should not be a compromising of his faith, but an attempt to understand the other person as a human being in the spirit of the Incarnation. It allows each to maintain his personhood, while granting the opportunity to share his faith. Interfaith witness is an integral part of the Christian-Muslim dialogue.

A concept of interfaith witness as an integral part of dialogue has been evolved by the Department of Interfaith Witness of the Home Mission Board, S.B.C. Dialogue, in this concept, serves the following purposes:

1) To help Southern Baptists to know what other groups believe, to understand and appreciate their beliefs in their own religion and culture.
2) To seek to establish contact and rapport with them on the basis of sincere, honest friendship.
3) To learn how to witness to them.[10]

In this concept of dialogue, listening may be more important than speaking, as each imparts his faith to the other.

Interfaith witness in dialogue is given by life-style as well as words. It includes identification with the Muslim in daily life. Dialogue involves the witness of a shared life, according to Montgomery Watt:

> The witness of a shared life is the primary aspect of mission . . . there is a place for the witness of words in the form of the assertion of positive truths. The person who has shared in the life of an alien culture, however, has been familiarizing himself with the thought-forms of that religio-culture. He is therefore better able to express the truths of his own religion in a form that the others will appreciate.[11]

The relationship of dialogue and interfaith witness is understood when dialogue is seen as a shared life. Dialogue, for the purposes of this guide, includes interfaith witness. It includes involvement in the life-situations of Muslim internationals, as well as discussion of matters of faith.

Historical Background of Christian-Muslim Dialogue

The history of relations between Christianity and Islam may be divided into three periods for the sake of this study. In the first two periods the relationship was more a confrontation than a dialogue.[12]

The first period began with the spread of Islam in the seventh century A.D. and continued until the beginning of the Crusades (c. 632-1095). Christian territories from the Middle East to Spain were conquered by Islam. The encounter between the two religions was affected by the intellectual superiority of Christianity and the military and political dominance of the Arab Muslims. Christian theologians and leaders defended their flocks from conversion to Islam by philosophical arguments. They attacked Islam as a Christian heresey. The most prominent leaders of this apologetical approach to Islam were John of Damascus (c. 675-749), Pope Leo III (d. 816), and Timothy the Patriarch (780-823). The nature of the encounter was polemical. There was little face-to-face confrontation. Most of the dialogue was carried on in hostile correspondence between Christian and Muslim leaders. The Christians often resorted to attacks on Islam and Muhammad to defend their faith against the accusations of Muslim leaders. The net result of this confrontation was to cause the Muslims to harden their stance toward the Gospel.

The second period began with the Crusades and ended in the beginning of the twentieth century (c. 1095-1906). Christianity launched a military and spiritual counter-attack to regain the Holy Land from the Muslims. The spiritual thrust was initiated from the monastic orders of Europe to win Muslims to Christianity by refuting the Quran. Peter the Venerable (d. 1156) sponsored a Latin translation of the Quran around 1141-43.[13] St. Francis of Assisi studied Islam and braved the Sultan's camp in Egypt to preach the Gospel to Muslims in 1219.[14] Ramon Lull, visionary and scholar, died as a martyr while on a mission to Muslims in 1316.[15] Concern for understanding Islam through the study of the Quran was re-awakened by Nicholas of Cusa in 1461-62.[16] This scholarly concern coupled with a deep desire to witness to Muslims with a view towards converting them set the stage for the nineteenth century giants in missions to Muslims; Henry Martyn, Cornelius Van Dyck, Karl Pfander and others. Some converts were won through the example of holy lives and disputation, but the results were, for the most part, meager and disappointing. Muslims tended to harden their resistance in the face of this spiritual assault.

A new approach to Islam began to emerge under the impact of the Enlightment. Radical scholars such as Relandus (1676-1718) began to call for a more objective assessment of Islam from original sources, rather than from prejudice. The defensive attitude toward Islam was altered under the influence of Louis Massignon (1883-1962) who had become a Christian through the study of the Muslim mystic and martyr, Hallaj.[17] Christian missionaries came to realize the futility of a frontal assult on Islam. A more honest and open approach of dialogue came onto the scene. This change was assessed by William W. Stennett:

> For years, because of the reasons given above, the manner of proclaiming the Gospel to the Moslem was primarily through argument. The missionary felt that he must by logical proof compel the intellectual acceptance of Christianity. This approach came to be known as "The Great Moslem Controversy." Some of its greatest adherents were men like Raymond Lull, Henry Martyn, Karl Pfander, and many others. They preached and wrote and though different in many respects, had confidence in an approach that had practically passed out of existence. Its passing began around the turn of the twentieth century. At the Cairo Conference in 1906 the controversial method was discussed and it was agreed that polemic should be avoided whenever possible, but that when it could not be avoided, it should always be conducted in the spirit of patience, fairness and love.[18]

This more open, dialogical approach to Muslims was pioneered by Canon Temple Gairdner (1873-1928) of the Anglican Church. It was popularized by the writings of Kenneth Cragg who issued the call to a retrieval of understanding, service, and patience in his book, **The Call of the Minaret.**[19]

The new stance of openness to non-Christian religions declared by the Roman Catholic Church at Vatican II in 1965 has had a positive effect on the Christian-Muslim dialogue.[20] Numerous dialogues have been reported in recent years between Christian and Muslim leaders. Christian-Muslim dialogues have been held in Ghana, Spain, Tunisia,[21] Cordova,[22] Hong Kong,[23] and in Tripoli.[24] Altogether, eight separate dialogues were sponsored by the World Council of Churches from 1966-1976.[25] These dialogues have dealt mainly with the common ground of both faiths and possibilities of mutual cooperation in fields of social, economic, and moral concerns.

Barriers to Dialogue with Muslims

One may question the practical value of formal dialogue between religious leaders and scholars for the average man in the street. Are these dialogues avoiding the real issues that separate Christianity and Islam? The Christian who meets a Muslim international in daily life soon becomes aware of the barriers to dialogue that must be faced on a very mundane level. Howe lists the common barriers to communication: language, images, anxieties, defenses, and contrary purposes.[26]. For the purpose of the Christian-Muslim dialogue we will summarize these into the four categories of language, culture, opposing beliefs, and monologue.

Language

The Christian finds that the first barrier to dialogue with Muslims is language or terminology. The Christian and Muslim do not mean the same things when such words as "sin" and "salvation" are used. In his study on sin and salvation in Islam, Charles Beckett, former missionary to Bangladesh, found that Islam denies original sin. Adam was deceived by Satan and immediately pardoned by God.[27] Sin does not wrong God but the sinner. It is usually a transgression of a ceremonial prohibition, or **dhanb**, which may be intentional or unintentional.[28] God provides cancellation of sin through actions, or obedience to ceremonial regulations.[29] The source of moral restraint in Islam is fear of God's judgment and the horrors of hell.[30] The Muslim's idea of sin and salvation is radically opposed to the Christian doctrine of atonement. Man, in Islam, is capable of saving himself if he so desires and thus needs no savior. The cross is denied in Islam because it is felt to be unnecessary and unjust.

Not only do the meaning of words differ, but the very purpose of speech itself is different for the Arab Muslim. The Arab almost worships the spoken word over the deed, as Morroe Berger describes:

> The Arab's incomplete emancipation from the groups that dominate him intensifies the lack of personal security resulting from casual child rearing, family instability, arbitrary rule, and poverty. His insecurity shows itself in a considerable amount of oral activity, in the relation between hospitality and hostility, in suspicion, and in a certain kind of extremism.
>
> The Arab's virtual obsession with oral functions can hardly escape notice; it strikes the observer in Arab reverence for language and oral arts as well as in the Arab attitude toward food. The richness of Arabic has had an almost bewitching effect upon those for whom it is the native language.[31]

Therefore, the Christian can find himself frustrated in dialogue with Muslims unless he knows the meaning that the Muslim attaches to the words used. Also he will find great difficulty with what the western mind regards as a complete lack of logic in the thought pattern of the Muslim.

Culture

The Muslim's language is a reflection of his culture. The typical Muslim lives in a country where religion, politics, and social relations are governed by Islamic law. His personal decisions are controlled by the extended family under patriarchal control. He is shocked by the individualism and moral laxness of western culture. He sees these as products of a basic weakness in the Christian faith. Christianity, to him, is a religion of the west, of Greece, Rome, and America. It is judged as inferior to Islam which has its roots in the Middle East.[32] The Muslim has great pride in his cultural heritage and is not always open to listen to what the Christian has to say about his faith.

Opposing Beliefs

The greatest barrier to dialogue between Christianity and Islam is opposing beliefs. Each views itself as the final religion revealed by God. Islam negates the central facts of Christianity; Jesus' death on the cross and his resurrection. Because of this crucial denial of the cross, Islam denies the atonement and holds a different view of the doctrine of God and man. It denies the Incarnation and the Trinity. The motivating force of Islamic morality is the fear of God's strict justice as opposed to the Christian concept of **agape** love.[33]

The Muslim denial of Jesus' death on the cross may have its origin in the heretical Christian sects of early Christianity.[34] Muhammad's negative reaction to the growing cult of Mary in the Christian churches of his day may have influenced Islam's denial of the Trinity and Incarnation.[35] Christians who are unaware of these denials find their efforts at dialogue and interfaith witness frustrated. The Muslim is frustrated, in turn, by the use of these concepts which offend him. This mutual disturbance is noted by Charles Malik:

> A Christian is disturbed, beyond and despite any simplicity of conviction, by the Islamic critique of Christianity, that the Holy Trinity is **shirk**, that the Crucifixion was only an apparition, that the stories about Christ and his Mother in the Koran are the authentic stories and not those in the four gospels, etc. Similarly, a Muslim must be disturbed, beyond and despite any beauty of simple conviction, by the Christian (implied) critique of Islam: that Christianity has not been abrogated by Islam, that God became man in Jesus of Nazareth without ceasing to be God, that this same Jesus actually died and rose from the dead on the third day, that the Church, as a distinct historic body, makes absolute claims about itself which imply fundamental criticisms of Islam, etc.[36]

Monologue

Failure to understand the barriers of language, culture, and opposing beliefs leads inevitably to monologue. Both the Christian and the Muslim fail to listen to what the other is saying and feeling. Each attempts to change the other's position through persuasion and attack on his religion. The negative forces of "The Great Controversy" are set into motion. The only way out of this dilemma is for the Christian to come to a deeper understanding of his own faith, as well as that of the Muslim. Virginia Cobb, deceased missionary to Muslims, described what should be our attitude as Christians toward Muslims:

> We are not warring with Islam . . .
> We are not debating with Islam to prove our views are correct and theirs incorrect . . .
> We are not trying to change anyone's religion . . .
> We need a stronger faith in the power of the truth . . .
> We need faith stronger in the reality of the living Christ...
> Our message is a Person we've experienced, not a doctrine,system, religion, book, church, ethic . . . Our faith in him is that once we lead a person to him, he will in direct contact with that person, transform and guide in all else.[37]

Cobb knew and experienced the truth that the only convincing witness to a Muslim was to live among his people in the spirit of the Incarnation. Dialogue, based on the Incarnation, is a shared life.

A Guide to Dialogue with Muslims

As a means of helping Christians to overcome barriers to dialogue with Muslims, a Guide to Dialogue with Muslims has been written, tested, and revised for this book. The original draft of the Guide was prepared early in the project and submitted to my doctoral committee on October 15, 1975. Additional copies were given to a select group of missionaries and laymen who are engaged in ministry to Muslims. Their comments were integrated into a revised edition of the Guide which was submitted at the end of the project.

The Guide is divided into two parts. The first part gives general guidelines to dialogue with Muslims. The second deals with typical questions asked and statements made by Muslims in conversations with Christians. Background information from Muslim traditions and the Quran is offered. An approach using the Quran and the Bible is suggested in dealing with the Muslim objections to Jesus' death on the cross and the Trinity. Argumentation is avoided. The objectives are to encourage the Muslim to a personal study of the Bible and to strengthen the Christian in sharing his testimony with the Muslim in an understandable way.

The style of the Guide is personal. It is written for the average Christian layman who meets a Muslim in the course of daily life. It is designed as a tool to encourage interfaith witness and dialogue through personal friendship with the Muslim. While the orientation of the writer had been with Palestinian Arab Muslims it is hoped that the approach of the Guide will be effective with Muslims in general.

III
GENERAL GUIDELINES TO DIALOGUE WITH MUSLIMS

The Muslim is generally an easy person to get to know. By upbringing he is friendly and sociable, especially to strangers. If he is an international in another country, he is lonely and needs friendship. It is not hard to enter into dialogue with a Muslim. Once he places his trust in you, you may find him to be a very expressive person for whom talking and debating comes easily. In fact, you will discover that a characteristic of the Middle Eastener, particularly the Arab, is the force with which an argument is pursued. It is the force of the argument, not necessarily the logic, which determines its validity. For this reason, a sense of humor and patience are prime virtues for you to acquire in dialogue with a Muslim.

Your first reaction to a discussion with a Muslim, particularly if he is a Palestinian Arab, may be to feel that you are being verbally "attacked"! He may launch into a political defense of the "Palestinian refugees" and an attack on the "unfair policies" of the United States towards the Arabs. If you will hear him patiently, he will probably apologize for his outburst. Then the way will be opened to a more personal discussion of matters of the spirit. The secret is not to get side-tracked by defending American foreign policy, even if you feel you should. This is sometimes difficult because the Muslim sees no separation between religion and politics. He assumes that a "Christian" nation should act differently from other nations. If you allow him to vent the trauma of his heart you may earn his friendship and be able to go on to share spiritual realities. You have then accomplished the first step in dialogue, which is to establish communication with the Muslim as a person.

Every Muslim is at a different stage in his commitment to the religion of Islam. He may be devout, that is; praying five times daily, abstaining from alcohol and pork, fasting for the Month of Ramadan, and committing parts of the Quran to memory. Or, he may be at the other end of the spectrum—an agnostic and materialist who feels that religion has no valid place in modern life. Your approach to dialogue on spiritual matters will depend on which place between these two extremes his spiritual interest lies. God, through his Holy Spirit, has created spiritual hunger in the hearts of many Muslims. However, he is likely to give a strong defense of Islam as a way of life even if he is a materialist and does not practice the rituals of Islam in daily life. He may defend Islam's superiority over the Christianity that he has observed in the United States and in other places in the western world. The best defense to such observations is to admit that some Christians do not live up to the highest precepts of their faith. The Muslim will most likely respond with the same confession about followers of his faith.

Before entering into dialogue about spiritual matters you have an obligation to learn as much as possible about the Quran, the history of Islam, and what the Muslims believe about Christianity. Several paperback editions of the Quran are available in English. You will be surprised to learn how much Christians have in common with Muslims. You will also note the crucial differences. By accepting the positive contributions of Islam, you will gain the respect and friendship of the Muslim. However, if you attack his religion, he will retaliate in the same manner. Comparison of the "good" in your religion with the "bad" in his is an exercise in futility. Let "dialogue" be a sharing of what is most meaningful in both of your lives. The Holy Spirit will lead you to discover what is beneficial from both of your faiths and will guide you in clarifying the difference.

It will be helpful to know that many of the teachings in the Quran resemble similar stories and precepts found in the Apocryphal or "non-canonical" New Testament writings. For instance, the stories of Jesus speaking and making bird from clay as an infant in Surah III:46, 59 are found in **The Gospel of Thomas the Israelite** and the Arabic **Gospel of the Infancy.**[1]

Some of its thoughts are also found in Jewish Talmudic literature. The source of other teachings strange to us are found in pre-Islamic history of the Arabian penisula.[2] According to Muslim tradition, Muhammad was illiterate. The Bible had not been translated into Arabic by his lifetime (d. 632 A.D.), as far as we know. He was dependent on oral tradition. His "revelations" which dealt with Christianity were conditioned by the theological disputes then occurring in the rival Christian denominations. These concerned mainly the divine and human nature of Christ and the place of Mary in the Incarnation. Muslim beliefs about the Bible and Christianity therefore have been conditioned by Muhammad's negative reaction to these disputes. Nevertheless, many common beliefs about Jesus are preserved in the Quran, such as his virgin birth, miracles, and ascension.

Three issues dominate the Muslim's attitude toward Christianity. First, he believes that Jews and Christians have deliberately distorted the Old and New Testaments to hide the predictions of the coming of Muhammad. Second, he assumes that the Christian believes in three gods. The Quran teaches that the Christians believe the Trinity to be composed of God, Mary, and Jesus. It rejects Jesus as the "Son of God." Third, he believes that Jesus did not die on the cross, but another such as Judas Iscariot or Simon of Cyrene, was crucified in his place.[3].

The Muslim's concept of sin and salvation is radically different than the concept of the New Testament. There is a great deal of confusion in Islam about what constitutes sin. The Quran is alternately severe and lenient in its attitude toward the punishment of sin. Sins, in Islam, are generally classified into two groups, capital and lesser sins. The tendency on the part of Muslim theologians has been to balance the severity of the Quran with God's complete forgiveness for all sins. The only exception is the sin of associating another god with God (Arabic-**shirk**).

Sin, to the average Muslim, is failure to live up to the standard of a moral code and failure to perform the requirements of the five "pillars of Islam." He feels that if he lives up to these ritual standards he is not a "sinner." He merits salvation by his good works which must balance his failures. Two angels record his good and bad deeds and these will be presented on the day of judgment.

However, the Muslim mystic fears hell fire, or purgatory. The fear motive permeates Islam. He knows that he has not lived up to all the requirements of his faith. He believes that no man can pay for another man's sins, so he must suffer for his own sins. He believes that Muslims will eventually be saved from purgatory by the intercession of Muhammad. However, the unbeliever who has associated any other god with God will suffer eternal punishment.[4]

The biblical concept of sin and salvation is contrary to that of the Muslim. The New Testament is clear in its teaching that all men are sinners and that Jesus Christ alone has the power to intercede on behalf of sinners because of his death on the cross and his resurrection from the dead. Salvation is by faith in Christ. It is a gift of God's love and grace and is not merited by any work that man can do.[5]

The Muslim's attitude towards what he believes that you believe about Christ is deeply engrained into his subconscious, and preconditions his attitude toward you and what you share with him. He feels that you have been deceived and he has an obligation to lead you to the truth of Islam. As you progress in dialogue, these differences will emerge, and you will have to deal with them. Chapter IV will cover some of the questions and statements he may use and will offer possible answers.

Remember, a primary obligation of dialogue is listening, as well as sharing. In listening you should try to hear what your Muslim friend is saying and feeling. Use listening as a time to learn from him what is meaningful in his life. If what he shares is unclear, ask him for clarification. You will then be free to share what is meaningful in your relationship with the Lord, and your understanding of the Bible. Your personal testimony will be more effective than any argument that can be offered to the truths that you hold. This will require much patience and time.

Several words of caution must be offered as you anticipate dialogue and interfaith witness with Muslims. The first is related to the method of approach. No other faith, not even Judaism, is so resistant to the "soul-winning" or "plan of salvation'' approach to witnessing. This approach is guided monologue which seeks to lead step-by-step to a ''decision for Christ.''[6] Even if the Muslim agrees to listen to this approach, which is highly unlikely, his ''confession of faith'' may be only a polite way to please, rather than offend you. It is very difficult to determine the motivation of his confession. Is he sincere? Does he expect financial gain or possibly a new wife? These are considered by some insincere Christians and Muslims in the Middle East as legitimate reasons to convert.

The real disadvantage to the ''plan of salvation'' approach is the confusion of terminololgy in the mind of the Muslim. As we have seen, words such as ''sin,'' ''salvation,'' ''Cross,'' and ''Son of God'' have an entirely different meaning for the Muslim. They fail to communicate the Gospel until the Muslim is better informed. In fact, they may even evoke a hostile response which defeats the purpose of their use. Chapter IV offers suggestions for an alternate approach using Scripture in a way that has been found more acceptable to the Muslim. Remember that the Muslim cannot see the meaning in our ''salvation'' terminology as long as he denies the fact that Jesus died on the cross.[7]

When discussing the Bible with a Muslim it is important that verses be read in their context. As will be seen, the Muslim has developed an intricate system of ''abrogation'' or substitution of one verse for another, due to the piecemeal way the Quran was written. He will have the tendency to try to find verses in the Bible that ''contradict'' each other. You will need to know the Scripture thoroughly. Lead him to understand the meaning of passages in relation to the setting in which they are found.

The Muslim will be impressed with your words only if he experiences your genuine friendship and sees you living a consistent moral life. Your Christian testimony must be matched by your lifestyle. The Muslim will be sensitive to the love and quality of life that Christ gives to you. Be sure to give the glory to God if the Muslim voices admiration for your Christian lifestyle. He will respect this as a sign of piety.

It is better to win the Muslim as a friend than to win an argument and lose his friendship. The history of Christian-Muslim encounter is full of argument, anger, and bloodshed. It is possible for the Christian to prove his case so well that he humiliates and inflames the Muslim. Communication can be broken and the purpose of dialogue defeated. Therefore, avoid critical remarks about Muhammad, the Quran, and Islam, even if he attacks your faith. Allow your patience and friendship to cause him to draw his own conclusions about the validity of your faith.

A word of caution must be made concerning your personal spiritual life. Dialogue with a Muslim can be a challenging and meaningful experience. However, it can be devastating if you do not maintain a close, personal relationship to God through Christ. Islam has an attracting power that appeals to human instincts. It appears rationalistic. However, its spirit runs counter to the love of God revealed in Christ because of the denial of the cross.

Dialogue with a Muslim will challenge your intellect and your spirit. It will cause you to rethink the very basis of your commitment to Christ. The result, after such testing, can be a deepening of your faith. Remember especially your need to maintain a consistent devotional life and to enlist the prayer support and fellowship of other Christians. The Holy Spirit can use this encounter to enrich your understanding of the Scriptures and the power of prayer. This can more than offset the difficulties you face.

A recognized possibility and danger for some persons in dialogue is the "conversion" of the Christian or Muslim to the faith of the other. This danger has more serious consequences for the Muslim. In Islam the threat of death may be used as a deterrent to conversion to Christianity. This subject will be discussed in Chapter VII.

Another word of caution must be made with regards to dialogue with a Muslim of the opposite sex. Most Muslims come from countries where contact with persons of the opposite sex is restricted until after engagement and marriage. Even engaged couples are chaperoned by family members. A strict, orthodox Muslim will not shake hands with or look a woman in the eyes, for fear of temptation. Therefore it is preferable that you relate to a Muslim of your own sex unless other persons are present. The freedom between sexes in the United States and other western countries can become the object of scorn for a Muslim when he returns to his home country. Make a point of learning the acceptable social norms of the Muslim lest he or she misunderstand your intentions.[8]

Pray for discernment, love, and patience in understanding your Muslim friend. Remember, he is also trying to understand you. Your willingness to understand his customs and to expose yourself to the Quran and the beliefs of Muslims will offer him an incentive to expose himself to your beliefs and to the Bible. It has been discovered by those working among Muslims in the Middle East that Christian friendship accompanied by a study of the Gospels constitutes the most powerful influence to acceptance of the Christian faith by the Muslim.

IV
QUESTIONS AND STATEMENTS ENCOUNTERED IN DIALOGUE WITH MUSLIMS

The following are some typical questions asked and statements made by Muslims to Christians in dialogue. Muslims are taught these questions as children in school. They know the answers generally given by Christians and are prepared for rebuttal. Rather than posing a threat to the Christian, these questions can be used as points of departure for meaningful dialogue and interfaith witness. As you begin dialogue with your Muslim friend, try to understand the feeling behind his questions. Relate them back to the Quran and clarify them with the Scripture. The following information is offered as resource material which may be helpful to you. It cannot be anything but a "Guide." The topics you discuss with a Muslim will more than likely not take the order in which they are presented here.

A. ON ISLAM

1. "Why are you not a Muslim?"

This question is often a form of a compliment. It is usually asked when the Muslim sees that you are interested in him and have taken the time to learn about Islam. He is also curious to know how anyone could resist the truth of Islam, which he believes to be God's final revelation to man.

My answer usually takes the following form: "I respect Islam as your religion, but I have surrendered my life to the will of God as revealed in Jesus Christ." This is not an evasion, for according to the Quran we read:

Surat al-Ma'ida (The Table) V:114:

> (The disciples of Jesus said) 'We have believed and we witness that we are Muslims.'

According to the Quran, Christians and all believers in God from Adam and Abraham are Muslims. Islam, like Christianity, is a personal faith in God that expresses itself in a life of surrender to the will of God. This same surah indicates that Jesus performed his great miracles by God's permission. His followers also live a life of submission to God. This is true Islam, or surrender to God's will. It is not a matter of denomination or nationality but a matter of obedience and trust in one's heart. Jesus revealed to us the basis of the life of submission to the will of God in John 6:38-40:

> For I have come down from heaven, not to do my own will, but the will of him who sent me: and this is the will of him who sent me, that I should lose nothing of all that he has given me, but raise it up at the last day. For this is the will of my Father, that every one who sees the Son and believes in him should have eternal life; and I will raise him up at the last day.

Jesus alone, according to the Quran and the Bible, has the power to raise the dead. It is God's will that all who believe in him should share in the resurrection. This resurrection is the ultimate hope of both Christian and Muslim.

2. *"What do you think about the Prophet Muhammad?"*

Islam, for the Muslim, implies belief in the one God, Allah, and in Muhammad as the final "seal of the prophets." Muslims have developed an aura of holiness around Muhammad. His every act as a man has set the pattern for the daily life of the devout Muslim. Despite the Muslim rejection of the diety of Christ, many in practice have unconsciously imputed his sinless character to Muhammad. Muhammad is looked upon by many as an intercessor between God and man. He is to them the ideal man, pure and sinless. Miracles were later ascribed to Muhammad, though according to the Quran no miracle is claimed except the revelation of the Quran itself:
Surat al-ᶜAnkabut (The Spider) XXIX:51:

> And it is not enough for them that we sent down to you the Book which is recited to them. Truly in that is a mercy and a reminder to the people who believe.

Because of this adoration of Muhammad it is unwise to make

any critical remark about him, even if supported by history. Such remarks will only anger the Muslim and cause him to attack you and Jesus. My answer is usually, "I respect Muhammad as your prophet. He led the Arab people from paganism to the belief in Allah, the one true God. But as a Christian, I follow Jesus. He revealed God's love to me by taking all my sins in his body on the cross. God raised him up. He is alive in heaven!"

The conversation usually goes one of two ways with this confession. First, the Muslim may begin to praise Jesus and begin reciting the story of his birth from the Quran. Or he might react by saying, "He did not die on the cross!" This leads naturally into discussion on the cross.

3. "Why do western Christians know so little about Islam?"

The Muslim, who has grown up in the Middle East where Islam is the dominant religion, is shocked to find that it is hardly known in the west. He assumes from his perspective that the world would be anxious to adopt his religion, since Islam is superior. In fact, he believes that every child is born a Muslim until someone changes his religion.

The Christian needs a basic knowledge of the rise and expansion of Islam to answer this question. The rapid advance of the Arab armies was halted in the East by Pope Leo III when the Muslim attack was repulsed at Constantinople in 717 and 718 A.D. In the West they were finally stopped by Charles Martel near Tours, France, in 732 A.D.[1] The Christians of Europe tried to regain the Holy Land during the Crusades. After several short occupations they were finally defeated by Muslims under Saladin in 1187 A.D. at the Horns of Hattin near the Sea of Galilee. The Christians were barely successful in holding back the invasion of the Ottoman Turkish armies into Europe in the 15th Century.

The historical answer to the question, "Why do western Christians know so little about Islam?", is that Christians in Europe prevented the spread of Islam into most of their territory. They remained Christian by choice. Our ancestors were Christians who immigrated to the west after the Reformation. Christianity is therefore the prevailing religion in the west to this day.

Christian-Muslim relations have been negatively influenced by this history of conflict. Both have tended to isolate themselves from an exposure to the other's faith. But the shrinking world of the modern age has forced us to take a more open stance toward each other. Dialogue can offer us the opportunity to share our faith, but it requires a willingness not to force the other to believe as we do.

An important point of general agreement for dialogue can be found in the Quran, **Surat al-Bakara** (The Cow) II:256:

> Let there be no compulsion in religion.

Neither Islam nor Christianity should compel belief by the sword, as was unfortunately the practice in the past. The Muslim **Jihad**, or "Holy War," had its unfortunate counterpart in the Crusades. True religion is a conviction of the heart and cannot be coerced. In dialogue, Muslims and Christians can challenge each other to serve mankind in peace and freedom.

The Muslim will be attracted to the ideal of religious freedom, which is lacking in many Middle Eastern countries where Islam is dominant. There a person is free only to remain in the religion of his birth or to convert to Islam. Conversion from Islam is punishable by death in some fanatical areas.

Ultimate freedom, for the Christian, is found only in spiritual regeneration through faith in Christ, described by Paul in Romans 8:2:

> For the law of the Spirit of life in Christ Jesus has set me free from the law of sin and death.

Encourage your Muslim friend to study the Bible and find the mutual points of agreement between your faiths in order that you may both share this freedom. Honor your friendship by becoming more informed about Islam. You will both benefit in the process.

B. ON THE SCRIPTURES

1. "Does not your Scriptures predict the coming of the Prophet Muhammad?"

Muhammad taught that his coming was predicted by the earlier Scriptures. He had expected both Christians and Jews to receive him as their new prophet in fulfillment of these predictions. When they refused, he responded by saying they had distorted their scripture (V:44).

The Muslim will quote the words of God to Moses in Deuternomy 18:18-19 in support of his question:

> I will raise up for them a prophet like you from among their brethren; and I will put my words in his mouth, and he shall speak to them all that I command him.

Muslims are led to believe that the "prophet" referred to in this passage from the Old Testament is Muhammad. Their commentators refer them to the Quran, **Surat al-Ahkaf** (Sand-Dunes) XLVI:10:

> The Children of Israel bore witness to the likeness (of this message).[2]

You can explain to your Muslim friend that Deuteronomy 18:18-19 was given by God to Moses in the Old Testament or **Tawrah** (Heb. "Torah") and according to the New Testament was fulfilled by the coming of Jesus six-hundred years before the Quran was written. This is confirmed in Acts 3:18-23:

> But what God foretold by the mouth of all prophets, that his Christ should suffer, he then fulfilled . . . that he may send the Christ appointed for you, Jesus, whom heaven must receive until the time for establishing all that God spoke by the mouth of his holy prophets from old. Moses said, "You shall listen to him in whatever he tells you. And it shall be that every soul that does not listen to that prophet shall be destroyed from the people . . . God having raised up his servant, sent him to you first, to bless you in turning every one from your wickedness.

Stephen repeated this prophecy in Acts 7:37 in his sermon before being martyred. Therefore, both Peter and Stephen affirm that Deuteronomy 18:18-19 refers directly to Jesus, the Messiah who was a Jew, "from among your brethren." It would have been impossible for this verse to refer to Muhammad because he was an Arab and a descendant of Ishmael.

Should your Muslim friend wish to pursue the subject further you can refer him to the New Tesament or the **Injil** (Gospel) where the Jews call Jesus the "Prophet" (Matthew 21:

11, Luke 1:76, 24:19, John 6:14, 7:40).

Ultimately, prophethood depends not only on the predictions of the prophet but on his character and works. The followers of Jesus could see clearly from his works that he was the one foretold in the Scripture.

2. The "Paraclete" Verses

The Muslim will point to the promise of the "paraclete," the comforter or advocate promised by Jesus in John 14:16, 15:26, and 16:7, as a prediction of the coming of Muhammad. The reasoning given by the Muslim is that his scholars teach that the Greek word **paracletos** is actually a corruption of **periclytos. Paracletos** means "an advocate, intercessor, councelor, comforter" or literally "one called to the side" to help us.[3] According to these scholars **periclytos,** when translated into Arabic, may be rendered **Ahmad,** the "Praised One", which is a name for the prophet Muhammad. A search of a Greek lexicon will show that the word **periclytos** does not exist in New Testament Greek! This word is obviously a fabrication from the Greek word **kleos,** "glory" or "praise."[4]

Encourage your Muslim friend to read the context of John 14:16. It will be seen immediately that the Counselor referred to here is the "Spirit of Truth" (v. 17) and plainly the Holy Spirit (v. 26). The same is true of John 15:26 and 16:7 when read in context. This Spirit of Truth is not a human being but the Holy Spirit whom Jesus will send from God the Father after he is raised from the dead. "He dwells with you and will be in you (John 14:17)."

The Muslim is led to believe that the "paraclete" refers to Muhammad because of commentaries on a verse in the Quran, **Surat as-Saff** (The Ranks) LXI:6:

> And when Jesus, son of Mary said, 'O children of Israel, I am the Apostle of God to you, confirming that which came before me from the Torah, and preaching good news of an apostle to come after me whose name is Ahmad.'

Interestingly this passage affirms that Jesus was the Apostle to the Jews who confirmed the law of Moses. This is an indirect answer to the question of the meaning of Deuternomy 18:18-19. The reference in the above passage to "an apostle" or "one sent," whose name shall be "Ahmad" or "be praised," according to the Gospel of John, chapters 14-16, refers to the Holy Spirit and not to Muhammad. Yusif Ali admits in the footnote mentioned above that the original word in the Greek text of John may have been **paracletos** rather than **periclytos.**[5] This observation by a knowledgeable Muslim scholar reveals the weakness of their argument. The **periclytos** theory simply cannot be proven.

One of the major characteristics of Islam is its inability to accept the personal reality of God revealed in the Holy Spirit. God in Islam can reveal himself only through intermediaries, or angels, who are created beings. Most Muslim scholars teach that the Holy Spirit was the angel Gabriel. In the case of the "paraclete" verses in John 14-16 they have deliberately avoided the context by trying to wring from these verses a prediction of the coming of Muhammad. Therefore use the opportunity to introduce them to the true "paraclete", the Holy Spirit, who Jesus gives to all who believe in him.

3. "Your Scripture has been corrupted!"

The Muslim contends that the "original Gospel" would certainly have predicted the coming of Muhammad. It would not have called Jesus the "Son of God." The Quran teaches that Jesus was not crucified. The Muslim believes that the original Gospel, or **Injil**, which God gave to Jesus, has been lost. Some Muslims say that the so-called **Gospel of Barnabas** is the true gospel.[6]

The idea of the corruption of the Christian Scriptures is common among the Muslims and has its source partly in the apparent contradictions between the Quran and the Bible. Proof is given by Muslim scholars of the many versions and apparent discrepancies in the copies of the manuscripts of the Bible. They often quote references from books written by Christian scholars who employ textual criticism.

It is necessary for the Christian to have a basic understanding of how the Quran came to be written that it may be compared with the Christian Scriptures. I do not advise discussing this with the Muslim unless he is open-minded. The average Muslim holds the Quran in such reverence that he might take great offense at the thought that there may have been more than one text of the Quran.

Muhammad's revelations were all delivered orally. His followers wrote them down on whatever material was available. There was no need for them to be collected until after his death in 632 A.D. Tradition related that Umar ibn-al-Khattab, who was to become Caliph in 634 A.D., went to Abu Bakr and suggested that the revelations be collected. Abu Bakr commissioned Zayd ibn-Thabit to do this. Zayd gathered portions of the Quran from 'pieces of papyrus, flat stones, palm-branches, shoulder-blades and ribs of animals, bits of leather, wooden tablets and the hearts of men.' After Abu Bakr's death this collection was given to Umar who entrusted it to his daughter Hafsa. In about 650 A.D. the Caliph Uthman commissioned Zayd and three Meccans to make another collection of the Quran using the materials of Hafsa. The new collection was completed, and certified copies of it were sent to the main centers of the Islamic empire. Instruction was given that all other texts were to be destroyed. It is this official "Uthmanic" text which is read by Muslims today.[7]

Most Muslim laymen are not aware that there were other versions of the Quran in existence in the beginning. They are quick to criticize the Bible for its many textual versions and variances. The fact is, that both in the case of the transmission of the Quran and the Bible, textual errors amount to an insignificant part of both books and do not alter any essential doctrine of either book.

Christians can be confident that the Bible has been transmitted accurately. For example, with the recent discovery of the Dead Sea Scrolls we have confirmation for the accuracy of the book of Isaiah in the Old Testament. The Isaiah scroll dates from about 125 B.C. and shows the unusual accuracy of the copyists who gave us the Massoretic text which dates over a thousand years later (916 A.D.). This beautiful Hebrew scroll is presently on display in Jerusalem.

One Bible scholar states that the Isaiah scrolls "proved to be word for word identical with our standard Hebrew Bible in more than 95% of the text. The 5% variation consisted chiefly of obvious slips of the pen and variations in spelling."[8]

The same degree of accuracy was maintained in the transmission of the New Testament manuscripts. No other ancient document has been so carefully preserved, as **The Interpreter's Bible** indicates:

> Since there exist more than fourteen hundred Greek manuscripts of the Gospels, ranging in date from the third century, down to modern times, not to mention lectionaries, large numbers of manuscripts of versions and many quotations of the church fathers, the text is extremely well attested. Although there is a rich wealth of variants, owing to both accidental and deliberate changes, the text is in good condition, and the true reading can often be established without difficulty. Frequently the choice of reading has some bearing on interpretation; yet it is probably true that no fundamental question of Christian faith and morals hinges on a disputed text.[9]

The editor of **Gospel Parallels** agrees that:

> . . . differences among the manuscripts . . . loom far larger than their actual significance should allow. The fact is that in about 90 per cent of the New Testament the manuscripts all agree; the differences occur in a small percentage, and do not affect fundamental Christian doctrine.[10]

It is obvious that the Muslims disposed of the problem of textual variances in the Quran by destroying all the texts but one. Christians, on the other hand, have preserved their variant texts knowing with certainty that the inspired message was not distorted through minor scribal error. We do well to remind ourselves and to testify to the Muslim that the true Gospel is not just the written Word, but the living Word, Jesus Christ himself! It is to him, and not to itself, that the Scriptures bear witness.

It may be better to defer the discussion of the technical issues involved in the transmission and development of the texts of the Quran and the Scriptures until the Muslim is ready to receive these. The real problem lies basically in the interpretation (tafsir) of the Books as we have them.

When your Muslim friend claims that "Your Scripture has been corrupted!," it is good to remind him of the verse in **Surat Ha Mim** XLI:43:

Nothing is said to thee that was not said to the apostles before thee.

Muhammad brought no new revelation, according to the Quran. He was simply a warner and a reminder of all that God had revealed in the **Tawrah** and **Injil**. This is confirmed in **Surat al-i-ᶜImran** (Family of Imran) III:3:

It is He who sent down to thee the Book in truth, confirming what went before it; And he sent down the Torah and the Gospel before this as a guide to the people, and he sent down the Furqan.

According to Muhammad the Quran confirms the **Torah** and the **Injil** (Gospel). Nowhere does the Quran say that these scriptures have been corrupted. In fact the Quran states that the Scriptures have been guarded from error, as we read in **Surat al-Ma'ida** (The Table) V:51:

And we sent down to you the Book in truth confirming the Book which came down before it and guarding it . . .

The mistaken idea that the Christian Scriptures have been corrupted may have come into popular Muslim thought through a misunderstanding of the technique of "abrogation" (an-nasikh wa-l-mansukh) which was used by Muhammad to substitute a passage in the Quran with a later revelation. This is described in **Surat an-Nahl** (The Bee) XVI:101:

If we exchange one verse for another, God knows what He sends down.

This is further clarified in **Surat al-Bakara** (The Cow) II:106:

We do not abrogate a verse or cause it to be forgotten unless we bring one better than it or like it. Do you not know that God has power over all things?"

Muslim commentators have justified these substitutions on the basis of "progressive revelation" and have developed an intricate system of dating verses in the Quran to determine which were revealed after other verses. The designation of "Meccan and Medinan" was attached to each Surah and in some cases to individual verses.

This leads us to a word of caution. Quoting from the Quran can be risky. The Muslim can often quote another proof text that has a contrary meaning. He will see no inconsistency in this. It is best to leave the burden of explanation of the Quran up to the Muslim. Knowledge of the contents of the Quran is valuable for the Christian in dialogue with Muslims, but it is better to hold that knowledge in reserve until the Muslim has had opportunity to present his view. Then lead him to the Scripture for further clarification.

There are accusations in the Quran that the Jews and Christians have twisted or hidden the meaning of their Scriptures. However, it does not charge that the texts have been changed.[11] The best approach is to assure your Muslim friend that God is true to his word and has guarded the Scriptures from any basic error. This is affirmed by Yusif Ali when he states:

> Muslims are therefore right in respecting the present Bible (New Testament and Old Testament), though they reject the peculiar doctrines taught by orthodox Christianity and Judaism.[12]

The respect for each others' Scripture as meaningful to each partner in dialogue will open the way to serious study of the Books. It is possible for the Christian to take the Quran seriously in the sense that it is the Book that motivates his Muslim friend to believe as he does. In doing so, he encourages the Muslim to take the Bible seriously. Each must agree that the texts of the books are valid as received with no major error in transmission. This does not bind either to accept the contents of the other's Book until he has studied it. Open inquiry is essential in dialogue and interfaith witness. The Christian can rest assured that the Bible will bear witness to God's revelation in Christ.

4. The Gospel of Barnabas

Muslims often support their accusation that the Bible has been corrupted by an appeal to the so-called **Gospel of Barnabas.** Most Muslims have never read this book but have heard of its existence from Muslim teachers. Their assumption is that the **Gospel of Barnabas** is the original Gospel given to Jesus by God and that our Gospels are forgeries because they do not predict the coming of Muhammad. It is necessary for the Christian to know something of the contents of this alleged Gospel to determine its value for the Christian-Muslim dialogue.

The present edition of **The Gospel of Barnabas** was published by the Quran Council of Pakistan in 1973 in celebration of the 1400th anniversary of the Quran.[13] Only 12,000 copies were published, making it a relatively difficult book to locate. The reason given for its publication is supposedly to promote better relations between Christians and Muslims in the spirit of the Roman Catholic Church's Second Vatican Council Declaration on "Religious Freedom" in 1965. As will be seen, the contents of the book discredit this intent.

The present **Gospel of Barnabas** was translated from an Italian manuscript in 1907 by Lonsdale and Laura Ragg. The publishers of the 1973 edition claim a long and colorful history for the manuscript beginning with Irenaeus (130-200 A.D.), a theologian of the early Church. However, a close check on this claim reveals that Irenaeus never quoted from the **Gospel of Barnabas** but from the non-canonical "Epistle of Barnabas."[14] James Cannon III of Duke University did an exhaustive study of the origin of the Italian manuscript and found that the earliest date that could be given to it was 1300 A.D., based on language, style, and content.[15] The Arabic version circulated in some middle Eastern countries is a translation from the Italian manuscript and not from an earlier Gospel.

The contents of the present **Gospel of Barnabas** reveal its Muslim origin. In it, Jesus denied that he is the Son of God and curses anyone who calls him the Son of God (53).[16] He is called the servant of God, not the Son of God (55). Jesus is not the Messiah (42) but predicts the coming of the Messiah, Muhammad, who is the Messenger of God (42-44). The Messiah is from the line of Ishmael and not from Isaac (43). It was Ishmael that Abraham offered up (44). Jesus sent out his disciples to undeceive the people who had come to believe him to be God (100). Jesus did not die on the cross but was taken up to heaven by four angels from the window of a house on the Mount of Olives (215). God cast the face and voice of Jesus upon Judas Iscariot who was then taken by the soldiers to be tried and crucified (216). The disciples came and stole the body and claimed that Jesus had risen from the dead (218). Jesus was brought back to earth by the angels to console Mary and the disciples and to tell them to wait for the coming of Muhammad (220). He was then carried back to heaven, but many of his disciples deceived men into thinking that he had died and risen again and others like Paul claimed he was the Son of God (222).

The technique of the author of this so-called "Gospel" is clear. The alleged author, Barnabas, is substituted for Thomas in the list of the twelve apostles (14). He gives Jesus the role of John the Baptist who then predicts the coming of Muhammad. He quotes freely from the four canonical Gospels, while inserting at will the Muslim traditions of 144,000 prophets (17), the fall of Satan (34), circumcision (22), and the contamination of the Christian Scriptures (124). The fear motive that pervades Islam is substituted for **agapé** love. He adds long, philosophical discourses on the nature of God, asceticism, predestination, and the after-life.

A glaring error of the author in this alleged "Gospel" is his obvious ignorance of the topography of Palestine. In section 20 we read, "Jesus went to the sea of Galilee, and having embarked in a ship sailed to his city of Nazareth." He rebukes the storm and, "Having arrived at the city of Nazareth the seaman spread through the city all that Jesus had wrought." The student of the Holy Land knows that Nazareth is in the Galilee Hills, 1300 feet above sea level, whereas the Sea of Galilee is over 600 feet below sea level! The author of the "Gospel of Barnabas" is obviously not the Apostle Barnabas of the New Testament but an Italian convert to Islam who never traveled to the Holy Land.[17]

The **Gospel of Barnabas** contradicts the Quran as well as the New Testament by its rejection of Jesus as the Messiah. The Quran states in **Surat al-i-ᶜImran** III:45, "His name is the Messiah, Jesus, the Son of Mary." It also disagrees with the Quran in claiming that the lineage of the Messiah was through Ishmael rather than Isaac. Finally, by giving the role of John the Baptist to Jesus it is in clear contradiction to the Quranic narrative of the birth of Jesus in **Surat al-i-ᶜImran** III:39, "God proclaims good news by Yehya (John) confirming a Word from God (Jesus)."

This so-called **Gospel of Barnabas** is obviously a forgery written to support the traditional Muslim views of the life of Jesus that developed after the time of Muhammad. Because it contradicts both the Quran and the Bible, it is unfit to be the subject matter of the Christian-Muslim dialogue. It is therefore unnecessary to mention its existence to the Muslim. Should he mention it, you can let him know that you are aware of its contents, but that it contradicts both the Quran and the Bible. You will most likely discover that you know much more about this "Gospel" than does your Muslim friend.

Encourage him to study with you the life of the true Gospel, which is Jesus Christ himself. His life is recorded in the four canonical Gospels which bear witness to him. Begin with the birth of Jesus and study the Sermon on the Mount. The questions and comments that arise will be the basis for continuing dialogue.

5. "Do you believe that the Quran is the Word of God?"

The Muslim holds the Quran in great reverence. Its recitation in the Arabic language has a captivating power over the listener. Muslims of many countries memorize portions in the Arabic language though they do not understand its meaning. Few Muslims will say that they understand the Quran. The sound of its recitation is in reality as sacred as its meaning for many Muslims. The Christian should be careful never to write on the text of the Quran or to place it on the floor, lest he offend the Muslim. Likewise we should treat the Bible with equal reverence in the presence of a Muslim.

The most tactful answer to this question may be, "The Quran is the Word of God for you, and I respect your belief." This question is difficult for the Christian especially if he has read the Quran and understands the areas where it radically disagrees with the Bible. If the Muslim presses further, answer, "I can agree with the Quran in every place that it agrees with the Bible, for the Quran claims to confirm what came before it in the **Torah** and **Injil**. As a Christian, I am required to believe in the inspiration of my Book." The inspiration in the Quran has been received from what God sent down before it, according to Surah III:3 and XLI:43. I assure the Muslim that God does not contradict himself. Then I encourage him to join me in a study of the Scripture in order that we may both know the will of God for our lives. Set an example for the Muslim by being a student of the Quran and the Bible. If he does not have a Bible give him a copy in his own language. Encourage him to read it and ask questions for clarification.[18]

C. ON THE TRINITY

1. "Why do Christians believe in three Gods?"

Our first reaction to this question is to answer, "We do not believe in three gods. We believe in one God who reveals himself in three ways." The nature of God is at the heart of the Christian-Muslim dialogue. For the Muslim, God is a numerical One who cannot be divided even to reveal himself to man. He is a king or sovereign who relates to men as his slaves. Man cannot relate personally to him but must submit to his arbitrary will. The prime motive of Islam is fear of God's strict justice rather than love for God. The Christian concept of God is that he is a God of love who desires to reveal himself to his wayward children. Through repentance and faith in Christ as God's self-revelation, man can restore friendship with his Creator. God is love and desires a free response of love.

We may assume that the Muslim's question is in reference to the Christian Trinity of Father, Son, and Holy Spirit. It is not. Muhammad's understanding of what Christians believed about the Trinity is entirely different as revealed in **Surat al-Ma'ida** (The Table) V:119:

> And then God said, 'O Jesus, son of Mary, did you say to the people', 'take me and my Mother as two gods apart from God?' He said, 'Glory be to you, I cannot say what is not my right to say!'

The trinity that Muhammad reports Jesus as rejecting was God, Mary, and Jesus, not the Christian Trinity of Father, Son, and Holy Spirit. The prominence of Mary in the worship and icons (images or pictures) of the Byzantine Church may have led to the assumption that she was on equal basis with Jesus and being worshipped as a god with him. The **Theotokos** formulation of the Creed of Chalcedon (A.D. 451) described Mary as "God-Bearer" or "Mother of God."[19] To Muhammad, belief in anyone beside God alone was idolatry, the unpardonable sin or **shirk.**

We too can agree with Muhammad that Jesus never intended for us to believe in himself and Mary as two gods. God alone is to be worshipped, through Jesus Christ, under the leadership of the Holy Spirit. It is necessary for us to describe our understanding of God as Father, Son, and Holy Spirit in a personal way. If these concepts of God have no personal meaning to us it is better to avoid using them with the Muslim. If we are humble enough to admit our own lack of understanding of this mystery we will be less likely to force these images upon the Muslim before he is ready to accept them. His inability to understand the love relationships of the Trinity stems from his rejection of Jesus' death on the cross. This will be discussed in Section D. 1.

We can agree with the Muslim about Mary. A Christian honors her, just as does the Muslim, as a morally pure person who yielded herself to the Holy Spirit and conceived Jesus, the Messiah. A dialogue on the Virgin Birth is a golden opportunity to read the story of the miraculous birth of Jesus in the Quran in **Surat Miryam** (Mary) XIX. You can compare this with the accounts in Luke 1-2 and Matthew 1-2. You will find that the Muslim agrees with you as you share these Scriptures together.

2. *"How can you say Jesus is the Son of God?" "God does not have a son!"*

The Muslim's rejection of the "sonship" of Jesus is based on several verses in the Quran,

Surat al-Jinn (The Spirits) LXXII:3:

> And the truth is that our Lord is exalted, He has not taken a female companion nor a son.

Surat al-Ikhlas (The Pure Faith) CXII:1-4:

> Say, God is one, the eternal refuge, He does not give birth, neither is he born, there is no one who can equal him.

Surat al-Ma'ida (The Table) V:19:

> They have indeed blasphemmed who say that God is Christ the Son of Mary.

Muhammad rejected the beliefs of the pagan Arabs who believed that God had sons and daughters. When he heard the Christians of his day calling Jesus the Son of God and Mary the "Mother of God," he exclaimed in **Surat Miryam** (Mary) **XIX**:35:

> It is not for God to take a son. Glory to him, if he wills a thing, He says to it, "Be," and it is!

Muhammad expressed what many Christians sense when faced with the mystery of the virgin birth. It is unexplainable. It was an act of God through the Holy Spirit. But one thing it was not. It was not the result of a physical act of intercourse between God and Mary. Muhammad rejected this, just as Christians do. This is stated clearly in **Surat al-Nisa'** (The Women) IV:171:

> Verily, the Messiah Jesus, son of Mary was an apostle of God and his word which he cast upon Mary and a spirit from him. Therefore believe in God and his prophets and do not say 'three.' It is better for you to be done with it! For God is one God. Far be it above him to have a son.

It is helpful to know that in the Arabic language there are two words for "son," **walad** and **ibin**. The Arabic word used in the Quran is "walad" which is a physical boy born as a result of the marriage of a man and woman. Muhammad rejected this thought as repugnant in regard to the birth of Jesus. It has the connotation of the pagan belief in the procreation of the gods. Unfortunately, Christians in his day had confused the issue by referring to Mary as the "God-bearer" or "Mother of God" (walidat-ila). To Muhammad this indicated that Christians believed she gave birth to God, or that God took for himself a son. To this day, the Muslim believes that Christians use "Son of God" as a title of physical relationship between Jesus and God. Therefore it is best to avoid the use of the term "Son of God" when beginning a conversation with a Muslim.

Luke 1:35 clarifies the Christian usage of "Son of God,"

> The Holy Spirit will come upon you, and the power of the Most High will overshadow you, therefore the child to be born will be called Holy, the Son of God.

The New Testament affirms, just as the Quran, that the birth of Jesus was caused by the coming of the Holy Spirit to Mary. It is not the result of physical intercourse. Therefore, the Arabic translation of the New Testament uses the word **ibin** for son rather than **walad**. **Ibin** is a title of relationship similar to the Old Testament usage of **ben**, "son of." It represents one who has a unique relationship with the Father, one who carried out the will of the Father and his purposes, and who therefore has a unique and supreme function of revelation.[20] Jesus is called the "Son of God," **ibin-Allah**, because of his relationship with God through the Holy Spirit. He was not the physical boy-child, **walad-Allah**, of God. The title, "Son of God," describes his spiritual relationship to God through the Holy Spirit. The key to an understanding of the Virgin Birth and the Sonship of Jesus is the Holy Spirit.

When explained in the above manner the Muslim will accept "sonship" as a relationship of obedience with the "heavenly Father." This relationship is described in John 5:30:

> I can do nothing on my own authority; as I hear, I judge, and my judgment is just, because I seek not my own will, but the will of him who sent me.

This is real submission, true Islam! For this reason the Christian gives Jesus the title of "Son of God." It is because he was always obedient to God, his heavenly Father, through the power of the Holy Spirit. We honor him no less than do our Muslim friends when they repeat **Surat al-i-ᶜImran** (Family of Imran) III:45:

> His name is the Messiah Jesus, son of Mary, Honored in this world and the next and among those who are close (to God).

The Muslim will agree that there is a sense in which we are all "children of God," **awlad-Allah**, through our common ancestry with Adam. But Jesus was unique because he was born of the Spirit of God, **min ruh-Allah**. Because of this, we can all become "Sons of God," **ibna-Allah**, through faith in Christ by repenting of our sins and receiving the Holy Spirit into our hearts. Our common weakness as human beings is the prideful and rebellious sin of the heart that prevents us from doing God's will. Sin is a perversion of God's image in man. The Muslim will understand this as the universal problem of the intentions of the heart (niyyah). Jesus alone can give us the Holy

Spirit that can remove the pride and rebellion from our hearts and help us to follow God's will. This revolves ultimately around an understanding of the cross which will be explained in Section D.

Admittedly the above explanation is best adapted to Muslims who are Arabic speaking, and is only one approach to a very large question. But it has also been found helpful with Muslims of Iranian background. Most Muslims have enough acquaintance with Arabic from their study of the Quran to understand the differences in the Arabic terms that are used.

3. "Jesus is only a Prophet."

The Muslim understands from the Quran that all prophets were sinless, or were "never false to their trusts" (III:101). This ideal is balanced by the idea they were "human like other men" (XIV:10-11). In this sense the Muslim would say that Jesus was not different from the other prophets who brought God's message to the people.

We can ask in return, "Was Jesus only a prophet or was he more than a prophet?" In the Quran there is strong indication that he was more than a prophet, as is revealed in **Surat al-Ma'idah** (The Table) V:113:

> Then God said, 'O Jesus, Son of Mary, remember my grace to you and to your mother when I confirmed you with the Holy Spirit so that you spoke to the people in infancy and maturity and when I taught you the Book and the Wisdom, and the Torah and the Gospel . . . and when you healed the blind and the leper by my permission, and when you raised the dead by my permission.'

Jesus is indeed unique in the Quran. Encourage your Muslim friend to believe all that the Quran says about Jesus—how he was born of a virgin, how he healed the sick, raised the dead, and how God gave him honor above all the prophets. Jesus alone, according to Muslim tradition, is "alive in heaven" (hayy fi-ssama'). Encourage him to read the similar accounts in the Gospels. He can reach his own conclusions about Jesus, whether he was a prophet or more than a prophet. Some Muslims come to the conclusion that Jesus was truly unique on the basis of a study of the Quran.[21]

D. ON THE CROSS

1. "Why do you say that Jesus died on the Cross? He did not die but another was substituted in his place."

The death of Jesus on the cross is the central issue in the Christian-Muslim dialogue. The cross is the pivotal point of history for Christians. Without the cross there can be no resurrection. Without the resurrection "your faith is in vain" (I Corinthians 15:14b). We have seen that the Muslim attitude toward sin is weakened by his failure to understand that sin is ultimately a perversion of man's will (niyyah). He believes that man can will to do right and can thereby please God. The denial of the cross is ultimately a denial that man is a sinner who has fallen short of God's image. In Islam man does not need a Savior other than God and God who has the power to forgive certainly would not become a man to bring salvation to men.

Admittedly, most Muslims have not thought through the implications of their denial of Jesus' death on the cross. They are not to be faulted that they were born into a religious system that denies the love of God as it is revealed in Jesus' death. The burden then lies upon the Christian to relate to the Muslim the truth of the cross in such a way that the Muslim can come to a new understanding of God's love revealed in the cross of Christ.

The Muslim's denial of Jesus' death on the cross is based on **Surat an-Nisa'** (The Women) IV:157-158:

> And they (the Jews) said, 'We killed the Messiah Jesus, Son of Mary, the Prophet of God.' And they did not kill him, and they did not crucify him, but it was made to appear to them. And those who disagree about this are full of doubt with regards to him. They do not have knowledge about this except to follow opinion. And they did not kill him at all, but God raised him up to himself. And God was powerful, wise.

Traditional Muslim interpretation of these verses teaches that God would not allow a sinless prophet like Jesus to be crucified. He tricked the Jews by casting Jesus' likeness or appearance upon Judas Iscariot, Simon of Cyrene, or someone from the crowd, who was crucified instead of Jesus. God raised Jesus up to himself. He is alive in heaven and will return to the earth someday to marry and have children. Then he will die and be judged with other men.

The Muslim will claim that this interpretation of the cross protects the honor of Jesus and the justice of God. But when one reflects on the subtle implications of a cross-less Christianity, he realizes how this undermines the very basis of the Gospel. One is led to ponder how the central event of the cross would have been twisted in the mind of Muhammad. Was it the influence of some heretical Christian sect that taught that Jesus only "appeared" to be a man? In the Gnostic **Acts of John** Jesus only "appears" to be crucified to the crowd and says, "neither am I he that is on the cross."[22] Or could it have been because Muhammad, in his most severe time of testing in Mecca, chose to flee for his life? In reality, the **Hijrah** was the very opposite of the cross. A religion based on the escape or **Hijrah** could not allow the cross to keep its meaning.

The Muslim argument for the substitution of another person in the place of Jesus on the cross hinges on the interpretation of the vague and mysterious phrase, "But it was made to appear to them." The Muslim will repeat this phrase in Arabic in any conversation on the cross, **"Wa lakin shubiha lahum."** He usually accepts the traditional interpretation of this verse without question. He does not realize that this interpretation contradicts several verses in the Quran that say that Jesus did die. Encourage him to study these other verses in the Quran: First, **Surat Miryam** (Mary) XIX:33:

> And peace be upon me the day that I was born,
> and the day that I die,
> and the day that I am sent back alive.

According to the Quran, this blessing was pronounced by the infant Jesus upon himself and shows clearly that he will die before being brought back to life.

Second, we read in **Surat al-i-ᶜImran** (The Family of Imran) III:55:

> God said, 'O Jesus, I will certainly put you to death and raise you up to myself.'

In this verse the Quran affirms that Jesus will be put to death (mutawaffyk) by God and then raised up.

Third, in **Surat-al-Ma'ida** (The Table) V:120, Jesus is made to say:

> When you put me to death (tawaffaytani) you were a watcher over them . . .

This thought is very close to the idea expressed in Isaiah 53:3, that the Messiah was "smitten by God."

Finally, the possibility of Jesus' death is shown in **Surat al-Ma'ida** (The Table) V:19:

> They blasphemed who said that God is the Messiah, Son of Mary!
> Say, 'who can defeat God in any matter, even if the Messiah, Son of Mary were destroyed . . .'

Here Muhammad rejects the idea that Mary is the Mother of God and clearly states that God's purpose cannot be defeated even if the Messiah is destroyed or crucified. In other words, God has the power to raise Jesus from the dead.

These verses throw light on the mysterious saying in **Surat an-Nisa'** IV:157-158. They show that the Jews thought they were killing the Messiah when they crucified Jesus, but God would not allow them victory in this evil act. They did not realize that in doing this they were actually fulfilling God's plan of putting Jesus to death for the sins of all mankind. In some mysterious way, God was responsible for the death of Jesus (III:55 V:120). Had he desired he could have saved Jesus from death. God won the victory at the cross by raising Jesus from the dead. The day is coming when all the "People of the Book" will believe in him, according to **Surat an-Nisa'** (The Women) IV:159:

> And there is none of the People of the Book that will not believe in him before he dies, and on the day of Resurrection he will be a witness against them.

The Muslim should be encouraged to read IV:157-158 in context. You might ask, "To whom was Muhammad referring when he said, 'They did not kill him, and they did not crucify him?' " The obvious answer from the context is, "The Jews." These verses vindicate God's victory over the cross by raising Jesus up to himself. They were never meant to be used against

Christians for their belief that Jesus died on the cross for the sins of the world. The misuse of these verses has deprived millions of Muslims of the knowledge of Jesus' death for their sins and caused needless division between Christians and Muslims through the ages.

Muslims who read and understand the meaning of the verses noted above are left with the dilemma of reconciling the death of Jesus with the statement in IV:157-158 that, "They did not kill him, and they did not crucify him, but it was made to appear to them." The mechanization of abrogation and progressive revelation is of no avail for it would mean setting aside a majority of verses on the death of Jesus, as well as the evidence of the New Testament.

A possible solution to the dilemma is found in that mysterious phrase, "It was made to appear to them," **shubiha lahum.** Muslim commentators have never been able to agree on what "appeared" to the Jews at the cross, to make them think they had killed the Messiah. Rather than pressing the Muslim with what appears to be a conflict in the Quran, I suggest that he turn with me to the Scriptures for the explanation. They reveal clearly what changed the "appearance," or in Arabic, **shibh**, of Jesus on the cross.

Admittedly the following explanation does not follow the usual Christian interpretation of what happened on the cross. However it must be realized that the concept of "It was made to appear to them," **shubiha lahum,** is deeply ingrained on the subconscious of the Muslim. It is whispered into his ears by his mother from infancy. The following approach has been found effective in helping the Muslim to understand the possibility of the cross in a new way. The traditional Muslim interpretation is that the appearance or **shibh** of Jesus was put on another person who was crucified instead of Jesus. The following alternative uses the Quranic term **shibh** but does not violate the meaning of the Scripture. I will follow the idea through the Scriptures to enable the Muslim to see that Jesus indeed died on the cross for him. This is how I would approach it:

What really happened on the cross? The Prophet Isaiah tells us that the Messiah's appearance would be marred beyond recognition, according to Isaiah 52:14:

As many were astonished at him—his appearance was so marred beyond human semblance, and his form beyond the sons of men.

He continues to describe what marred the Messiah's appearance (53:3-4):

Surely he has borne our griefs and carried our sorrows. Yet we esteemed him stricken, smitten of God, and afflicted. But he was wounded for our transgressions, He was bruised for our iniquities.

The Apostle Peter quotes freely from Isaiah 53 as he describes the suffering of Christ (I Peter 2:22; 24):

He committed no sin; no guile was found on his lips. When he was reviled, he did not revile in return; When he suffered he did not threaten; but he trusted to him who judges justly. He himself bore our sins in his body on the tree, that we might die to sin and live to righteousness. By his wounds you have been healed.

It comes as no surprise that New Testament writers quote at least thirty times from Isaiah 52 and 53 as they look back upon the death of Jesus. As Henry Shires relates in **Finding the Old Testament in the New,**

Many more parallels could be given, but these should suffice to demonstrate that as the N.T. writers sought ways of interpreting the life, and especially the death of Jesus, they utilized almost every verse of the main Suffering Servant passage of Isaiah.[23]

The Scriptures reveal that the appearance of the Messiah would be marred beyond human recognition because of his suffering for our sins. It would seem as though God himself had destroyed him. This is very close in meaning to the verses in the Quran noted earlier (III:55 V:19 and V:20). The appearance or **shibh** of Jesus was changed beyond human recognition by his suffering for the sins of mankind.

The Arabic translation of the New Testament uses the Arabic root of the word **shibh** in a number of verses that refer to the suffering of Jesus. In every case this word is used in some way to describe the death of Jesus on the cross.

The Epistle to the Hebrews in chapter two relates why Jesus

had to suffer death. He tasted death as the only perfect representative of humanity. He was made perfect through suffering and partook of human nature, that through death he might destroy the power of the Devil who had the power of death (v:14). In Hebrews 2:17 we read:

> Therefore he had to **be made like his brethren** (yushbiha ikhwatahu) in every respect, so that he might become a merciful and faithful high priest in the service of God, to make expiation for the sins of the people.

In his humanity, Jesus was made like his brethren (yushbiha ikhwatahu), the Jews, to fulfill God's plan. In his sacrificial death he was more than a man. He was a high priest who, because of his perfect manhood, was able to pay the sin penalty of all men through the shedding of his blood. Therefore God raised him up and crowned him with glory and honor (v. 9).

The Muslim who has accepted the cross as a historical event can come to appreciate the implications of the sacrifice of Christ. Blood sacrifice is still a part of the ritual practice of Islam on the religious holiday of **ᶜId al-Adha** and the pilgrimage or **Hajj** where sheep and goats are slaughtered.

Another verse in the New Testament reveals that Jesus' likeness (shibh) was that of sinful flesh and sin, so that in his death he could free us from the law of sin and death; Romans 8:1-4:

> For there is therefore now no condemnation for those who are in Christ Jesus. For the law of the Spirit of life in Christ Jesus has set me free from the law of sin and death. For God has done what the law, weakened by the flesh, could not do: sending his own son **in the likeness of sinful flesh and for sin,** (fi shibhi jasadi-l-khatiyyati), he condemned sin in the flesh, in order that the just requirements of the law might be fulfilled in us, who walk not according to the flesh but according to the Spirit.

Jesus was the only one who could die for our sins because he was the only pure, sinless man who was born of the Spirit of God and who had the Spirit of life dwelling in himself. The justice of God is revealed not by escape from the cross, but by Christ condemning sin by taking our sins in his body and dying for us. Granted, this is a mystery that is understood only when the Muslim has his heart enlightened through faith in Christ and his death on the cross.

Another verse employing the use of **shibh** or "likeness" in the Arabic text is that magnificent passage of the glory of God in the humiliated Christ, to whom every knee shall bow; Phillipians 2:6:

> Who, though he was in the form of God, did not count equality with God a thing to be grasped, but emptied himself, taking the form of a servant, being born in the **likeness of men**, (shibhi-nnass). And being found in human form he humbled himself and became obedient unto death, even death on a cross.

Here again we see that Jesus' likeness or appearance (shibh) was that of a man, the servant of God, bearing the sins of humanity. Because of his willingness to submit to the will of God, he was "highly exalted" (v. 9), or as the Quran has said, "Honored both in this life and the life to come" (XIII:45). That is the reason that, according to Phillipians 3:9 and **Surat an-Nisa'** IV: 157, "God raised him up." True Islam, or submission to God's will, is found in the humility and obedience of Jesus on the cross.

Finally, the likeness or appearance (shibh) on the cross was a picture of death. Jesus was identified with the sin and death of every man when he died on the cross. This death is symbolized in the act of believer's baptism in Romans 6:5:

> For if we have been united with him **in a death like his** (bi shibhi mawtihi) we shall certainly be united with him in a resurrection like his.

Both the Christian and the Muslim hope to share in this resurrection. The day of judgment (yawm ad-din) is a prominent teaching in Islam. Everyone who understands what Jesus did on the cross and accepts his death for his sins can perform this act to identify with him in his death. By faith in Christ we receive the same Spirit that raised him from the dead (Romans 8:11). This is the mystery hidden in the **shubiha lahum** passage in **Surat an-Nisa'** IV:157.

An understanding of this mystery can unite both Christians and Muslims through dialogue. According to Romans 8:29,

God is calling all men, "to be **conformed to the image of his son** (mushabihina surat-ibnihi), in order that he might be the first-born among many brethren." True dialogue will lead us both to a new understanding of Christ and unite us as brethren. For true dialogue can open both in a new way to the Spirit that unites us and enables us to re-interpret those truths that once separated us.

Experience has shown that the Muslim can also be brought into a new understanding of the cross through clarification of the difference in the work of Jesus' body and the work of the Spirit. Two verses that have proven effective for this clarification are:

1. Luke 23:46:

   And Jesus cried out with a loud voice and said, 'Oh Father, into thy hands I commit my spirit. And when he said this **he breathed his last** (surrendered up the spirit, Arabic: aslam ar-ruh).

2. I Peter 3:18:

   For Christ also died for sins once for all, **being put to death in the flesh, but made alive in the Spirit** (mumatan fi-l-jasad walakin muhyan fi-rruh).

Jesus bore our sins in his body on the cross, but he surrendered his Spirit to God. I Peter 2:24 says, "He himself bore our sins in his body on the tree." We have seen that his body was marred beyond recognition because of sin and suffering according to Isaiah 52:14. He surrendered up his Spirit to God. That same Spirit returned to him and raised up his dead body on the third day. We can agree with the Muslim that, "He is alive in heaven!" (hu hayy fi-ssama'). Because he is alive in heaven he is able to send the Holy Spirit from God to everyone who believes, in keeping with his promises in John 14-16.

The foregoing approach to the death of Christ has been effective in explaining the cross to Muslims who know Arabic. Some have remarked that, "For the first time in my life I understand what happened on the cross!" It is possible that you will have to adapt another approach in keeping with your own understanding of the cross. Your personal testimony of how you came to understand the meaning of the cross will be most meaningful to him. It is important that the approach communicate spiritual truth in the thought-forms of the Muslim. It is essential that the Muslim comes to believe in the fact of Jesus' death, before he can understand the spiritual implications of that death for himself. Only then will other Christian terminology such as "Son of God," "Savior," and "Lord" have real meaning to him.

These verses can be shared with him over a process of many sessions. It will be difficult for him to absorb their meaning in one sitting.

In the dialogue process, you will find your own concepts of the oneness of God in relationship to Jesus and the Holy Spirit being challenged and clarified. You will begin seeing new implications of the oneness of God in the Scriptures that perhaps you had not seen before. The mystery of the cross and the resurrection will take on new meaning as the Holy Spirit enlightens your mind. In other words, you will grow in the process of dialogue, along with your Muslim friend.

E. ON THE CHURCH

1. "Why is Christianity divided?"

The Muslim asks this question partly out of rebuke and partly from bewilderment. The rebuke is upon a divided Christianity. Admittedly the Muslim usually overlooks the various divisions within the Islamic community. But in dialogue with a Christian he will maintain that, "Because God is one, his people should be one!" His bewilderment comes when he sees the high degree of independence of western Christians, even within some denominations. He is actually confused by the different names of churches on the same street. Disagreement between denominations supports his belief that God allows dispute in order to distinguish the believers from the unbelievers, as can be seen in **Surat Hud** XI:118-119:

> And if your Lord had willed he would have made the people one nation, but they do not cease to disagree, Except for those on whom the Lord had mercy, And for that he created them. And the Word of the Lord was fulfilled; That 'I will fill Hell with the jinn and the people altogether.'

The Muslim does not see denominations within their historical framework. He is also unaccumstomed to the freedom of differing expressions found in western churches. The petty bickering of some Christians over fine points of theology adds to his confusion. When representatives of opposing denominations find themselves as an insignificant minority in a Muslim country, they discover that they no longer have the dubious luxury of disagreeing over unessentials.

Unfortunately, the lines of theological division among the Christian communities in the Middle East are drawn even finer than in the United States. The theological formulas that created divisions in the churches of the East in the third and fourth centuries are still repeated in the prayers of these churches in the twentieth century. This means that if you discuss Jesus with a Muslim in the presence of Christians from the traditional churches, you may find these Christians disagreeing among themselves as to the nature of Christ. Muslims see this as a confirmation of Muhammad's objections to Christian disputation over the nature of Christ in the Trinity.

With this caution in mind, it is imperative that we, as Christians, be united in the common desire to share Christ with the Muslim when we engage in dialogue. This common desire will enable us to put aside unessential points at which we may disagree among ourselves. One of the most disheartening experiences is to see Christians disputing among themselves over fine points of theology in the presence of Muslims. It is good to agree among yourselves as to who will be the spokesman of the group. This will be respected by the Muslim because it is his custom to defer all discussion to his leader or **sheikh**.

When discussing the Church with a Muslim it is best to emphasize the basic unity of all Christians in matters of faith and doctrine. The average Muslim sees the Roman Catholics, Greek Orthodox, and Protestants as one community. He may have had pleasant experiences with priests, nuns, and missionaries in mission hospitals and schools in his home country. Therefore, it is best to honor this witness of other denominational servants and try to build upon it. Should he have had an unpleasant experience with any of these, one must rebuild a relationship of trust that will magnify Christ and the written

Word. In the process you will confirm for him the words of **Surat al-Ma'ida** (The Table) V:85:

> And you will find the nearest of them in love for those who believe, those who say, 'We are Christians!'

In relating to Muslims as members of the Church we should abide by the prayer of Jesus in John 17:20-21:

> I do not pray for these only, but for those who are to believe in me through their word, that they may all be one; even as thou Father, art in me, and I in thee, that they also may be in us, so that the world may believe that thou has sent me.

Today, there are indications that God is uniting Christians of all denominations in a bond of fellowship, worship, and love. Revival is being reported from many lands. Muslims are being touched by the spirit of love that issues out of true renewal. Those who visit in the west will be more impressed when the spirit of competition gives way to a spirit of trust and unity in the Spirit of Christ. Then the same warmth of fellowship that we feel for each other will empower us for dialogue and interfaith witness with Muslims.

2. "Why do Christians love the Jews?"

This question is loaded with intense feeling because of the current Arab-Israeli conflict over the Palestinian Issue. Many of those who ask this question have lost home, land, and family members in the conflict in the Middle East. It is impossible to avoid this question if you are seeking to dialogue with Muslims, particularly if they are Arabs. Tact and wisdom are necessary. It must be remembered that the Jew also expects total support for his viewpoint. In a real sense the Christian is "caught in the middle." This may be God's design to enable us to be messengers of reconciliation.

First, I point out that we as Christians are suppose to love the Jews. We are commanded by Jesus to love even our enemies (Matthew 5:44). According to our Scriptures and the Quran (II:83) the Jews are God's covenant people. Jesus, the Messiah, was a Jew. The Arab Muslim usually retorts, "And they crucified your Messiah! (unconsciously admitting that he was crucified). How could you love such a person?" This brings us to the heart of the Gospel message; that God is love and he sent Jesus to die for the Jew and all men, for their salvation (Romans 1:16). I, as a Christian, must love the Jew, the Arab, and all persons. It is true that the Jews have from time to time been disobedient to the covenant of God. The orthodox Jew will tell you this. However it is not for me as a man to judge as only God can judge.

Many Christians have studied the Bible since they were children in Sunday School and church. It is natural for Christians to have feelings of kinship for the Jewish people and strong ties with the Holy Land. Some Christians see the return of the Jewish people to the Holy Land as a fulfillment of prophecy. The Arab Muslim responds, "I do not agree with the persecution of the Jews, but why does he have to return at my expense?" As was mentioned earlier, I allow him to vent the trauma of his heart.

A denounciation of the Jews is found in the Quran, due to their rejection of Muhammad as a prophet in Mecca and Medina. For instance we read in **Surat al-Ma'ida** (The Table) V:85:

> You will find that the strongest enemies to those who believe are the Jews and pagans.

Both Jews and Christians are denounced in **Surat al-Ma'ida** for turning away from the teachings of their Scriptures and prophets and forming alliances with each other (V:54-74). Because of what Muhammad considered as treachery by the Jews, the direction of prayer, the **kiblah** was changed from Jerusalem to Mecca. Muslim tradition substituted Ishmael for Isaac as Abraham's favorite son.

Remind your Muslim friend as long as a spirit of hatred remains between Muslim, Jew and Christian, peace can never be achieved. Forgiveness is required. Unfortunately, the spirit of forgiveness is found neither in the Muslim nor in the Jew. Retribution continues to deepen hatred. A miracle of God's love and forgiveness must break the cycle of hatred. Share with your Muslim friend the story of the crucifixion where Jesus said, "Father forgive them for they know not what they do." (Luke 23:34). Experience has shown that both Muslim and Jew can love and forgive each other when their hearts are changed by the Spirit of Jesus.

It is naive for us to envision a lasting solution to the Middle East problem until man's nature is radically changed. Neither Muslim nor Jew believes in Jesus as personal Savior and Lord. This fact is often forgotten by Christians who take sides on this delicate political issue. It is my deep personal conviction that Jesus' death on the cross and the fruit of the Holy Spirit, received by faith through the power of his resurrection, alone provide the motivating power for this radical change of attitude. Seething hatreds erupt periodically in the Middle East plunging the world to the brink of war. The conflict between Arab and Jew offers the Christian his greatest challenge—to be a peacemaker and reconciler of men. To know the answer and fail to share it is to be unfaithful to the objective of dialogue, which is the miracle of reconciliation.[24]

There are things that the Christian can do to bring reconciliation whether in the Middle East or in America. He can invite his Muslim and Jewish friends to share a social time in his home. The Christian Arab can play a vital part in such encounters. Topics of mutual interest can be discussed. Experience shows that it takes a year or more of socializing for the Arab and Jew to come to the place of trust that will enable them to share their real feelings. The Christian's presence offers a buffer for the hostilities that may erupt. However, friendships can be formed through such meetings that affect social and business relations in the community. Admittedly, attempts to bring reconciliation are not always understood by those who are politically oriented. However, this risk is one that must be taken by a messenger of reconciliation.

It may come as a surprise that Muslims and Jews sometimes work together, live near each other, and socialize at weddings. There have been periods of history when Muslim governments have been tolerant of Jews. It is when the larger issue of the political conflict enters that hostilities erupt. The Arabs have a proverb that is injected into political discussions that brings a smile and a change of subject: "Politics is like a stubborn billy goat!" (as-siyyasi tayyasi). It reflects the general mood that no ultimate solution for man's problems can be found in man's blundering. The Christian alone has the secret of the Gospel that must be made known through dialogue with both Muslim and Jew. God alone can change men through the miracle of dialogue which leads to reconciliation. He can use you as a messenger of this reconciliation.

V
SUMMARY OF GUIDELINES FOR DIALOGUE AND INTERFAITH WITNESS WITH MUSLIMS

You may ask, "What can I do to encourage dialogue and interfaith witness with Muslims?" The following are some general guidelines that have been found helpful in relating to Muslims:

1. It is wise to learn as much as possible about the religion and culture of Islam. Study the history of the Muslim's country. Learn the simple greetings in his language. Visit in his home and invite him to yours. The Muslim is usually a very sociable person. An excellent book to introduce you to the Arab and Muslim people is by Morroe Berger, **The Arab World Today**, (Anchor Books, 1964). Other books and information about witness with Muslims can be received from "Fellowship of Faith for Muslims" (FFM), 205 Yonge Street, Room 25, Toronto, Ontario, Canada M5B 1N2.

2. Have on hand a copy of the Bible and the Quran. **Good News for Modern Man** is helpful for Muslims with limited English. However, if he has studied in a mission school he may prefer the more classical King James Version. Obtain a copy of the Bible or New Testament in Arabic or his native language from the Bible Society or your mission board. **The Quran Interpreted** by A. J. Arberry (Macmillan: 1974) is very readable and can be obtained in paperback through your local bookstore. If possible, obtain a copy of the Quran in Arabic with English interpretation. Treat the Bible and Quran with respect in the presence of the Muslim. Never lay it on the floor, or write in it.

3. Dialogue is a two-way conversation in which each listens to the other. Therefore, allow the Muslim to give you his views. Listen to his feelings as well as his words. Let him quote from

the Quran. Ask him for his own personal explanation, not just that of a commentator. Then share with him what you believe and what the Bible says on the subject. Let him read the Bible in his own language. Encourage him to read entire chapters in order to understand the context. Offer him a copy of the Bible and read it with him when you visit him.

4. You will win the Muslim's friendship by agreeing with him on things you hold in common, such as belief in one God, the creation, and the Virgin Birth. However, avoid argumentation. Never make disparaging remarks about Islam, Muhammad, or the Quran, even if he attacks your faith. He may do this to test your patience and love. If you retaliate, you are no better than he is. Encourage him to study the Bible and come to his own conclustions. Be ready to answer his questions using the Bible as your resource.

5. It is best to deal with Muslims of your own sex. Customs in Muslim countries limit social contact to persons of one's own sex. Learn the Muslim's social standards. Let him know you respect these.

6. Terms such as "Son of God," "Lord," and the "Trinity" are offensive to the Muslim. "Lord" (Arabic: rabb) is a term Muslims use only for God. Use instead terms with which he can relate, such as "Messiah," "The Word of God," and the "One born of the Spirit." Avoid arguments on the Trinity. Describe the Holy Spirit in personal terms that have meaning to you, but not in mathematical formulas. Remember, until he believes that Jesus died on the cross for him, he will not understand these other terms.

7. Remember to pray for him and with him concerning any personal problems. Keep his confidence. You may be one of the few persons he trusts. Do not share what he tells you with others without his permission.

8. It is best to avoid quoting from the Quran until after you have read and studied the whole book. As a Christian, you are expected to be an authority on the Bible, not on the Quran. The Quran often takes a positive and negative stance on the same subject. Also, various versions of the Quran have a different numbering system for the verses which may lead to confusion. If the Muslim does quote from the Quran, you may use the references given in this Guide to remind him that there

are other possible alternatives to the verses that he commonly uses.

9. Share your personal testimony of what Christ means to you in a natural way. Explain the circumstances that led you to trust Christ. Let him know how it changed your attitude toward God, the Bible, and other people. He may respond that you were "born a Christian." Explain your understanding of the necessity of the "new birth," "confession," "salvation," and "eternal life" from passages which have meaning to you (i.e. John 1:12-13, John 3:1-15, Romans 3:23, 5:8, 6:23, 10:9-10, Ephesians 2:8-10). You will discover in the process the points at which he agrees or disagrees. Refer to Section IV for clarification. Remember, the Muslim's ability to absorb these new ideas may be limited, depending on his background. You will need patience. Try to understand his concepts and his objections in the process. The most natural setting for this sharing is in the midst of the ordinary day by day events of visits, meals, and trips together as friends. Remember, God, not you, is the one who converts the heart. In the process of dialogue, you also can expect to be "converted" to new understandings of spiritual realities as your faith is challenged. Your unconditional friendship may be, in the final analysis, your most valuable contribution to dialogue and interfaith witness with a Muslim.

10. Invite your Muslim friend to your church on special occasions such as Christmas, Thanksgiving, and Easter. He will enjoy musicals, plays, and social events. He will want to know the meaning of various acts of worship. The questions that arise from these visits will give opportunities for further dialogue. If you are in an area where there is a Mosque, ask if you can observe a prayer service. Customarily, shoes are removed before entering the sanctuary. Women pray in a special section, usually the balcony, out of sight of the men.

VI
WHAT TO DO FOR PERSONS WHO DECIDE TO CHANGE THEIR FAITH

A. A CHRISTIAN WHO CONTEMPLATES CONVERSION TO ISLAM.

Dialogue is communication between two or more people. In the Christian-Muslim context it is sharing of truth or reality as each has experienced it. It is a search for solutions to the differences that separate the faiths. In dialogue there is the possibility that either party may decide to change their minds regarding their faith. The fact of history is that both Christians and Muslims have changed their faith. In a particular country in the Middle East there was concern on the part of the authorities in recent years over the growing number of Christians who were converting to Islam in order to marry Muslims or to get better jobs. These persons were in their opinion not "denying their faith" to take this step. In the atmosphere of growing secularism they were simply going through a necessary expedient in order to gain a more satisfying life-style, or to meet some personal desire. We may question their motivations. However, the Spirit of Christ would cause us to look with compassion on them.

You may know Christians who have contemplated conversion in order to marry a Muslim. It is our obligation to relate to them in love and patience, just as we would to a Muslim. It could be that the failure of the Church to be a loving and nurturing fellowship contributed to their decision.

What can you do for the Christian who appears ready to compromise his faith and join Islam for the sake of marriage? (A woman can remain a Christian to marry a Muslim, but a man would be required to convert to Islam to marry a Muslim woman.) First, provide this person with information such as is found in this Guide. Trust God to lead them to a correct decision. Islam can look very logical and enticing to a potential convert. Therefore provide information about the life of Muhammad, the Quran, and Muslim social customs that will provide a better basis for his or her decision. Share the spiritual realities of Christianity in the process and assure the person of your concern and prayers, no matter what the final decision may be.

Second, provide spiritual encouragement through counsel and prayer. One has to have endured the same turmoil of mind and heart to understand what that person is enduring in this crisis time of life. Maintain fellowship and encourage them to remain consistent in worship and prayer with a supportive group of Christian believers. A person often becomes entangled in such a dilemma from the motivation of converting the Muslim to Christianity, only to find that the sexual attraction adds an unexpected complication, making a rational decision very difficult. Be firm in the scriptural counsel that mixed marriages with persons of differing religious beliefs are strictly forbidden in the Old Testament (Genesis 24:3, 28:1, Deuteronomy 7:3, Joshua 23:12, Ezra 9:12, Nehemiah 13:25). Admittedly, this prohibition deals with marriage between Jews and pagan Gentiles of another age. Nevertheless, I believe it contains an element of cautionary wisdom that is applicable in the Christian-Muslim context today. Paul also warns of the consequences of marriage to unbelievers (I Corinthians 7, II Corinthians 6:14-7:1). However, these warnings must be given with love and tact, lest the result be to drive the persons into a hasty decision to marry before he or she has a change of mind!

One of the best deterrents to mixed marriage is the counsel of Christians who have married Muslims or other persons from different cultures than their own. Most have found the adjustments extremely difficult and are anxious to warn others not to enter the same predicament.

Remember, it must be their decision. If they maintain control over their physical desires they could have a positive influence over the Muslim. But there is a period in the process when the outcome is very uncertain. Prayer and understanding are much needed.

What should be our attitude toward the Christian who has married a Muslim despite counsel to the contrary? This has brought serious adjustments into the Christian's life-style. Relatives are often embittered on both sides of the family. There have been periods of loneliness and uncertainty in foreign lands. Such persons should be the objects of the continuing ministry of the church both in America and overseas. They should be counseled to love their mates and raise their children with care. These persons may be the contact point for their mates and their children coming to know about Christ, though marriage should not be entered into with this uncertain objective in mind. God has unusual ways of opening the door to dialogue and interfaith witness, even through Christians married to Muslims, providing we are sensitive to the opportunities.

B. THE MUSLIM WHO DECIDES TO BE A FOLLOWER OF CHRIST.

A growing number of Muslims, after prolonged exposure to the Christian message, are indicating a desire to become followers of Christ. They are discovering that Christ alone fills the void in their hearts and brings them into relationship with God as a loving heavenly Father. Unfortunately, the Church is not always ready to receive and nurture them. In the Middle East the Muslim has been unwelcome in many Christian churches because of the fear of false motives and the open hostility of the Muslim community. However, God is revitalizing the Church and causing many congregations to become vital fellowships to believers. The Muslim is being attracted to this spiritual vitality. Christians are losing their fear of witnessing to the Muslim.

Muslims are travelling to the west for work and study. They are curious about the prosperity and influence of the many churches they see. Americans are finding that the "mission field" has moved into their neighborhood. They are finding unexpected opportunities for dialogue and interfaith witness with Muslims in their own hometown. Christians can trust God to make them "ministers of reconciliation." He will empower us for interfaith witness. Through us the Muslim can be drawn to him who "enlightens every man" (John 1:9).

What can we do for the Muslim who decides to follow Christ? First, we can be aware of the mixed motivations that may lead to his decision. Seldom are any of our motives completely pure in major decisions in life. A period of testing of motives is usual in the beginning of the Muslim's decision. He wants to know if your motives are pure. If he finds that you will yield to using money or other enticements to get him to "convert," he will lose respect for you. As we test motives it is good to remember that the Muslim has little to gain and much to lose should he make a clear-cut decision to follow Christ. If he finds you are sincere in your trust in Christ he will have more confidence in trusting you with his spiritual nurture.

Second, the Muslim needs to know he can trust you. Therefore, keep his confidence. Do not share what he has told you in private, even with your own husband or wife, unless he gives you permission to do so. Distrust and suspicion are an integral part of the fear motive which governs Islamic society. Introduce him to Christians who can be trusted to keep his confidence. Let him be the one to share his testimony of faith in Christ. Remember, he could lose his family, his job, and even his life if we are indiscreet in announcing his new found faith.

Third, the Muslim who accepts Christ will have a need for personal Bible study. You can be of real encouragement by acting as a resource person for his many questions as he begins a study of the scripture. Share your own personal experiences as you study these meaningful chapters together. The Sermon on the Mount (Matthew 5-7), The Gospel of John and the Epistle to the Hebrews are excellent resource materials. The Muslim will be impressed by the apocalyptic literature in Ezekiel, Daniel, Matthew 24, and the Book of Revelation. These are similar in content and style to the Quran. The Epistle of James will attract him by its admonitions. The parables of the Kingdom in the Gospels will impress him. The empowering of the Church for witness in the Acts of the Apostles will give him encouragement as he begins to experience the work of the Holy Spirit in his own life. He will identify with the Psalms as he endures persecution and hostility. The Bible is your resource book. He may need a copy in his own language. He will appreciate your being prepared to answer his questions and to follow the lead of his interests.

Fourth, as a friend, you will want to know his or her family situation. Encourage him to witness discreetly to his family by sharing his new discoveries in the Scripture. If he feels it wise, visit in his home and make friends with his family. He will want his family to be united with him in his new-found faith. This is extremely important in order that he will not be isloated from his family and culture. In many areas of the world, as well as in America, Muslims are willing for their children to receive Bible training. They respect the moral contributions of the Bible and the wholesome atmosphere of Christian schools.

Fifth, pray with him and for him at every opportunity. Teach him how to pray using the Lord's prayer as a model. Be sensitive to his moods. The Muslim often receives insights through dreams and visions. You will be asked to help him interpret these. You should use the Scriptures as the basis for any interpretation. Islam has incorporated elements of the occult from pre-Islamic paganism in Arabia. You will learn to take seriously what the Bible has to say about the spirit world as you share the thoughts of the Muslim. These manifestations are real to him. Encourage him to accept the victory of Christ over the demonic forces in his life. This is appropriated through prayer, confession, and the fellowship of discerning Christians.

Sixth, encourage him to become a part of a fellowship that will nurture his spiritual growth. You may have to encourage fellow Christians to receive the Muslim. He will be sensitive to their acceptance or their suspicions. It may be better to begin with a smaller prayer or Bible study group where he can find acceptance. If there are other Muslims nearby who also indicate a desire to follow Christ, these could be encouraged to band together for study and prayer. Experience in Muslim lands is showing that most Muslims do not feel comfortable in the more westernized Christian churches. He will probably prefer groups of other Muslim believers who share his life-style and thought patterns.[1]

Finally, let him make his own decision about believer's baptism. He will discover Christ's teachings about baptism as he studies the Scriptures. Public baptism or conversion in some countries of the Middle East can result in severe persecution.

The Muslim can be threatened with loss of family, job, and even his life. Some will request "secret baptism." This usually means that only those whom he trusts and who have had an influence on his spiritual pilgrimage would be present. If the Muslim has had a genuine experience of trust in Christ and his life has evidenced the change that Christ brings, his request for baptism should be honored. The Ethiopian eunuch was baptized in a foreign country with Phillip as the only witness as far as we know (Acts 8:26-40). It is vitally important that we know that there is a group of trusted believers with whom he can have fellowship. This problem is not as severe in America where Christianity is the predominant religion. Entire Muslim families have joined churches through baptism in the west. However, baptism is only the first decisive step in Christian growth. The Muslim needs our fellowship even more after baptism as he adjusts to the changes in his lifestyle. Many have become discouraged, returned to Islam, or lost all interest in religion when spiritual growth is not sustained.

A renewed emphasis on the ministry of the Holy Spirit in the life of the believer is adding spiritual vigor to the churches. It is of utmost importance that the Muslim sense the unity of the Holy Spirit between various churches. The fellowship that issues from this unity will provide an atmosphere for continuing spiritual growth in his life.

CONCLUSIONS

Numerous opportunities are available to the Christian to share his faith with Muslims around the world today. Our countries are international communities. Muslims from many nations are a vital segment of this international scene, on college campuses, in business, and in the community. The modern sophisticated Muslim in a secular society will not be content with a monologue in which the Christian tells him what to believe. However, he will be willing to engage in dialogue. In dialogue, both the Muslim and the Christian share their witness in an atmosphere of friendship. The Muslim is a person who expresses his faith. He will expect you to share your faith with him.

Dialogue is basically a ministry of reconciliation and an attempt to communicate truth. Barriers to communication can be overcome by listening to the Muslim's objections and restating our beliefs in terms that communicate meaning to the Muslim. The Quran and the Bible are the resource books for the dialogue.

Dialogue assumes the risks involved in being open to the other's faith. The Christian who feels led to turn to Islam must be treated with compassion and counseled with wisdom. The Muslim who wishes to become a follower of Christ should be nurtured through fellowship and love. Unity in the Holy Spirit is essential between persons and denominations who engage in dialogue with Muslims. This unity will provide a fellowship in which the Muslim can grow in his understanding of Christ.

Dialogue is not for the weak in faith, but for those who are strong enough to become "all things to all men that some might be saved" (I Corinthians 9:22). Dialogue is a call to be messengers of reconciliation between the adherants of two faiths that have often opposed each other while claiming to worship the same God. It leads naturally to interfaith witness. It is an investment of friendship with Muslims that will not go unrewarded. In dialogue we are challenged to trust God. He alone has the power to change the Muslim. He has changed us. That is all the assurance we need.

APPENDIX I
A SAMPLE MINISTRY TO MUSLIMS IN THE U.S.A.

SETTING FOR MINISTRY TO MUSLIMS

Muslims in the United States

Muslims are becoming an integral part of the pluralistic religious scene in the United States. A quest for education, employment and political asylum has brought an estimated two million to our shores. This increasing Muslim presence has been a matter of concern for both the Home and Foreign Mission Boards (H.M.B. and F.M.B.) of the Southern Baptist Convention. The Home Mission Board through its Department of Interfaith Witness has been anxious to test methods of approach to Arabic-speaking Muslims in order to determine the most effective means of ministering to this growing ethnic group. The Foreign Mission Board was anxious for one of its representatives to be involved in a pilot project of evangelism with Muslims. Both concerns and my personal calling to dialogue and interfaith witness with Muslims coalesced to form the motivation for the project of a Christian ministry of dialogue with Muslims.

Need for an Arabic Language Ministry— Campus and Community

During my furlough in 1974 I met an Arab Muslim family in Eastern North Carolina who in turn introduced me to the Arab Club at North Carolina State University (N.C.S.U.), in which over 100 Arab students and their families participated. 178 Muslim students were enrolled on campuses in Raleigh. 40 Arab families lived in town. I attended Arab Club meetings, and learned that they were anxious to create a more positive image of the Arab than was generally held by the American public. Members of the International Student Board (I.S.B.)

desired to understand the Arab mentality. There was also an openness at the Baptist Campus Ministries to create a climate for ministries to internationals. The Baptist State Convention had been studying the possibility of hiring a staff person to work among internationals. There was an obvious need for a facilitator of dialogue with Muslims on campus and in the community.

Background Studies on International Ministries

A pioneer project in ministry among internationals in the Research Triangle area of North Carolina was completed by Dr. George W. Braswell, Jr., in May 1973.[1] A continuing ministry to internationals was developed in 1974 by Rudolph Malcolm Wood.[2] Both Braswell and Wood observed that a project in ministry to internationals may best be accomplished among national groupings. They also noted that internationals are interested in religion, but are sensitive to attempts to proselyte them. Churches and campus organizations were hesitant to become involved with internationals because of lack of persons sufficiently qualified and motivated to minister to specific language groups. Regret was expressed that the F.M.B. did not sufficiently utilize the talents of furloughing missionaries to reach internationals. Their observations encouraged me to begin a ministry specifically to Arabic-speaking Muslims through the Arab Club at N.C.S.U.

Objectives, Methodology and Testing

My first objective was to contact Muslims and engage in dialogue and interfaith witness with them. This would be accomplished through attending Arab Club and Muslim Student Association (M.S.A.) meetings, to be followed up by invitations to my home and after personal visitation in their homes and dormitory rooms. Establishing friendships that would lead to Christian-Muslim dialogue was a priority. This would be tested by the keeping of a diary, a file of contacts, and an evaluation by persons involved in international student ministries.

The second objective was to serve as a resource person on Islam and as a facilitator of dialogue with Muslims in campus organizations and churches in the community. I planned to accomplish this through training sessions with interested students, to be followed by an "Arab Night" at the Baptist Student

Center where Christian students could become acquainted with Muslim students. Also, I would participate in International Student Retreats and activities of the denomination to determine the value of the program for Christian-Muslim dialogue. This role would be tested through evaluations by the campus directors.

The third objective was to write and test a "Guide to Dialogue with Muslims" which would serve as a training tool and resource for myself and others engaged in ministry to Muslims. It would be practical and personal and usable by the average Christian layman who meets Muslim internationals in the community. Selected professors, missionaries, laymen, and a Muslim would evaluate it.

The above objectives, testing and evaluation were submitted as a project for my Doctor of Ministry degree program at Southeastern Baptist Theological Seminary.

Base of Financial and Spiritual Support

Both the Home and Foreign Mission Boards cooperated to sponsor the project and enabled me to take a one-year extension of furlough. The Hayes-Barton Baptist Church in Raleigh offered me their facilities, resources of their Benevolence Committee, and spiritual support for the project.

DIALOGUE OPPORTUNITIES THROUGH CAMPUS MINISTRIES

It was felt in the beginning of the project that the international student organizations would provide the natural contact points for meeting Arab students. The Baptist Student Center, located at the edge of the N.C.S.U. campus, would provide the corresponding organization from the churches.

The first phase to initiate dialogue was a training session to acquaint Baptist students with Arab culture and Muslim beliefs. I was assisted in this by a Palestinian Arab student who was an officer of the I.S.B. He gave a humorous account of his adjustments as a newcomer to the U.S.A. and I presented a brief summary of the history of Islam and the Christian-Muslim dialogue. Following a brief period of discussion, the students were led in a series of communication games to help the students to experience the frustrations faced by internationals in a strange culture.

Unfortunately, second phase plan for an "Arab Night" at the student center was thwarted. We had planned a program highlighting "The Cultural Similarities of the Kiowa Indians and the Palestinians." The Arab Club leader, who was an Egyptian, was hesitant to accept the invitation for fear of any possible political stances that might seem to be projected. The Arab Club and the I.S.B. had come under criticism for an earlier program that presented the Palestinian issue. It was obvious that to pursue the matter would be to ride a line of division in the Arab Club. I recommended that the "Arab Night" function be cancelled.

Muslim Student Association Banquet a Success

Unknown to me, the Muslim Student Association (M.S.A.) was planning its celebration of the end of the Fast of Ramadan on the same night that I had proposed the "Arab Night." They were having difficulty in finding a place to meet. I recommended that the Baptist Student Center be made available to them.

I attended with my wife and an Egyptian Muslim friend. Over 125 Muslims were present. A speaker from an Islamic Center in Texas spoke on the theme "The Ideal Man and the Educational Goals of Islam." At the banquet I was able to meet Muslim student leaders who were very helpful to me in preparing the "Guide to Dialogue." Also, an American girl who was engaged to an Iranian Muslim provided me with a copy of the **Gospel of Barnabas,** which was used in preparing the "Guide."[3]

As a result of attending the M.S.A. banquet, I was invited to Quran studies at the N.C.S.U. Student Center on Sundays and to eat at the home of an officer of the M.S.A. who was a devout Shi'ite Muslim from Iran.

International Student Conference at Thanksgiving

I attended this conference at Chowan College and met twelve Saudi Arabian students from the English Language Service at Sacred Heart College in Belmont, North Carolina. Coincidentally, I met a pastor of a church in Charlotte, who referred me to one of his church members who was a student at Sacred Heart. This student used the "Guide to Dialogue" in discussion with these students at the college and found it very helpful.

Inter-Varsity (I.V.) Christian Fellowship

I.V. had the most active ministry to internationals at N.C.S.U. The director, Mrs. Bette McGee, hosted internationals in her home in Cary in cooperation with I.V. and the local Presbyterian Church. I.V. was sensitive to the international students' social needs in its presentation of the Gospel. It prepared student volunteers specifically for ministry to internationals. I attended the annual international picnic at the Presbyterian Church, and was able to meet Muslim students in a relaxed atmosphere. Later I was invited to speak at an International supper at the McGee home in Cary. Of the seventy students present, twelve were Muslim. My topic was "The Holy Spirit in the Life of Jesus." I dealt with the death of Jesus and the Trinity. In later discussion the Muslim students indicated that it helped to clarify some of their misunderstanding.

At a later I.V. international dinner, I invited a Christian Arab friend to attend with two Muslim friends. The Christian was surprised at the openness of the Muslims to dialogue over coffee in their room after the meeting. Application of ideas in the "Guide" had prepared the way.

The I.V. excelled in training and in an open and honest presentation of the Gospel message in word and deed. However, I noted that an aggressive and conservative theological stance tended to drive some conservative Muslims into a defense of Islam. If not tempered with an understanding of Islam, this approach can be counterproductive with Muslims.

DIALOGUE OPPORTUNITIES IN THE COMMUNITY

About forty Arab families resided in Raleigh at the time of this project (1975-6). Most had immigrated to the U.S.A. after 1948 and had relatives in other parts of the state. Their only real social cohesiveness, aside from family ties, was attendance at Arab Club functions at N.C.S.U. I was able to befriend a number of these and serve as an unofficial pastor-counselor and as a liaison with the local churches.

Friends in Market-places and By-ways

Variety was added to this project by numerous contacts

with Muslims while shopping, attending ball games, and traveling. Listening to personal problems of these people created opportunities for sharing a word of encouragement or a deed of service. Trust was developed over a period of time which led to Christian-Muslim dialogue in a number of cases.

At a local restaurant, it was discovered that the three employees were Arabs from Lebanon; a Muslim, a Christian, and Druze. One remarked, "If we were in Lebanon today, we would be shooting each other!" At the high school soccer games, I met an Arab physician whose son played on the soccer team with my son. Our sons enjoyed fooling their opponents by calling out their strategies in Arabic. On a plane trip to Atlanta, I met a young business executive, a Shi'ite Muslim from Iran, who later read a New Testament I gave him. Later, at a homecoming football game in Virginia, I became acquainted with an Arab Muslim psychiatrist who invited me and a local pastor friend to lunch. An Iranian government official bought a Bible in a Christian bookstore one day and was referred to me by a friendly clerk. These chance meetings of Muslims led me to see:

First: My availability and interest in personal encounters with Muslims was a key factor in capitalizing on these opportunities. As my interest became known, more opportunities developed.

Second: It was important to relate these Muslims to some trusted Christian in the local community.

Third: The value of these contacts for the Christian-Muslim dialogue depended on the theological awareness of the Muslims, and were conditioned by their personal problems. My contact was a link in a chain of their prior acquaintances with Christians.

Americans Married to Muslims

During this project I met seven Americans married to Muslims. Six out of the seven were marriages of Muslim men to Christian women. The first couple I met while preaching at my former church in Eastern North Carolina. The wife was a former Baptist who had converted to Islam. They sent their children to a Christian boarding school in the Middle East to save them from the perversion of the American youth culture. I was invited to their home for dinner. The wife asked me to explain the meaning of John 3:16 to her husband in Arabic so he could share this central truth of Christianity.

Another Baptist lady contacted me after I appeared on a local television station during a World Missions Conference. Her husband was an Arab Muslim professor teaching in the local university. She was anxious to know how to share her faith with her husband.

Because of these and other acquaintances with Americans married to Muslims, I incorporated a new section into the "Guide" dealing with conversion to Islam. While not recommending mixed marriages, I have come to see that these do offer opportunities for dialogue and interfaith witness with Muslims if the Christian partner exercises love and patience.

Foreign Missions Lead to Home Missions

A number of Muslims who settle in American have received a favorable impression of Christianity in Christian mission schools in their home countries. This lays the foundation for Christian-Muslim dialogue. The father of one Muslim family had worked with a Quaker school in the Middle East. He and his children were very open to friendship and dialogue. Though he had identified with a Christian church in America, his basic theology had changed very little, and the cross was still a major barrier to a full acceptance of the Gospel.

A group of laymen attended a Foreign Missions Conference at Ridgecrest. As a result of our meeting there, they returned to their home town and began ministry among Christian and Muslim Arab doctors in a local hospital. I was later invited to lead a training session on Christian-Muslim dialogue and interfaith witness in their city.

Social Ministry as a Part of Dialogue

Dialogue as a shared life led me to assist two Muslims with serious financial problems. The first was a young Muslim woman who had been divorced and left with a young child and only minimum child support. Although well educated in her home country, she was forced to work as a part-time seamstress here. My wife was able to get some financial aid from the Benevolence Committee of our church. I assisted her in applying for food stamps and arranged a job interview for her. Subsequently her financial situation improved.

A Muslim student who was a Palestinian refugee from Lebanon was unable to receive money from his parents due to fighting there. I tried to help him obtain food stamps, but he was refused because of his student status. The church Benevolence Committee gave him a small grant. He was very helpful in opening up good relations with the members of the Arab Club.

These experiences helped me to see that Muslims, as other internationals, do not have access to financial aid available to those living in the community, or do not have knowledge of how to obtain aid. It is an act of Christian compassion to assist these persons in acquiring legitimate aid. Personal loans or gifts are a last resort, as these tend to make the person feel under obligation to the donor. Muslims are hesitant to receive financial assistance until all other sources are exhausted. Personal pride is a vital factor. When applied properly, financial aid can restore a person's confidence and build a trust relationship that opens the way to dialogue and interfaith witness.

The Home as a Setting for Dialogue

Our home became a relaxed setting for dialogue as the project progressed. Muslim students were invited as dinner guests for Thanksgiving and other occasions. These invitations were always returned. In every case I found Muslims open to discuss their faith and to respond to an explanation of my faith. An invitation for a meal is a sign of trust and friendship to an Arab Muslim. Likewise, it is important to accept his hospitality in return.

However, I discovered that it is wise to invite only one Muslim at a time if the intention is to enter into dialogue on theological subjects. On one occasion two Muslim students who were invited to my home disagreed with each other to such an extent that it was difficult to enter into dialogue to any degree! The element of suspicion and hostility can be so prevalent that it is a matter of wisdom to deal with each individually. Especially is it important to keep the Muslim's confidence and not disclose to others what he has shared with you.

The Church as a Part of the Community

As friendships were developed with Muslims, I invited them to attend services at my church. Church attendance by Muslims was not regarded as a goal of the project. However, it was introduced as a natural way to become better acquainted with the American community. The response on the part of Muslims was usually positive, especially for "community" events such as Wednesday night suppers and youth fellowships.

On one occasion, three Palestinian Arab Muslims were invited to an adult Sunday School class dinner, and asked to share their views on the Middle East situation. They were pleased with the freedom they were given to share their thoughts. In turn, one asked, "What makes the Baptists different from other Christian churches?" This opened the way to share our distinctives and the bond we have with other Christian believers.

Attendance of Muslims in worship services and fellowship activities enabled Muslims to experience Christian fellowship and increased their curiosity about the distinctives of our particular denomination. It also introduced church members to Muslims and encouraged them in a continuing ministry to Muslims in the community and on campus.

A note of caution was learned: in about half the cases Muslims failed to keep appointments to church events. It is very important to check with them by telephone the day of the appointment and pick them up personally. In each case the Muslim apologized for his failure to keep an engagement. Patience and persistence are virtues. The rewards more than offset the occasional disappointments.

MINISTRY OF DIALOGUE WITH MUSLIMS EVALUATED

The objectives of this ministry were threefold: (1) to engage in a personal ministry of dialogue with Muslims, (2) to act as a resource person to facilitate dialogue between Christians and Muslims, and (3) to write, test, and revise a Guide to Dialogue with Muslims. In order to gain objectivity in evaluating the results of this project, I asked four persons familiar with my ministry in the town/university complex of Raleigh to respond to the following questions:

1. What is your evaluation of the writer as a "facilitator of dialogue" with Muslims? Has he been effective as a resource person on the religion of Islam and Middle East Culture?

2. How has this ministry contributed to your own life with respect to relationships with Muslims?
3. The Guide to Dialogue with Muslims:
   Did it increase your knowledge of Islam?
   Did it help you in your own dialogue or witnessing with Muslims?
   Is the revision a sufficient clarification of your original comments on the first draft?
4. Do you feel there is an opportunity for a similar ministry in the future?

Personal Ministry of Dialogue with Muslims

During the six months of concentration on this project in ministry I made personal contact with over two-hundred Muslims in North and South Carolina. As contact proliferated it was deemed necessary to concentrate on about twelve individuals who showed willingness to engage in dialogue. The principle of selection, as described in Robert E. Coleman's book, **The Master Plan of Evangelism**, was seen to be necessary and valid for this ministry:

> . . . One can not transform a world except as individuals in the world are transformed, and individuals cannot be changed except as they are molded in the hands of the Master. The necessity is apparent not only to select a few laymen, but to keep the group small enough to be able to work effectively with them.
>
> Hence, as the company of followers around Jesus increased, it became necessary by the middle of His second year of ministry to narrow the select company to a more manageable number . . .[4]

Work with Muslims is slowed by the necessity of working with each individually rather than in a group. It was to my definite advantage that I was granted an additional year of furlough allowing more time to individuals, especially during the last six months.

The methodology of making contact with Muslims through campus organizations, particularly the Arab Club and the M.S.A., proved effective. Arab Palestinians responded readily to invitations to my home and these visits paved the way to their attendance at church-related functions. The effectiveness of this ministry increased as I came to know these individuals better.

The keeping of a diary and a file of contacts provided continuity to this phase of ministry. Reading through the diary served as a reminder of opportunities for follow-up with individuals for dialogue.

My theological presuppositions for the Christian-Muslim dialogue were tested and found in need of clarification:

1. I was able to confirm that the Muslim's understanding of the nature of God affects his outlook on life, as well as his receptivity to the Christian message. For instance, the Muslim conceives of God as a numerical One and has great difficulty conceiving of him in trinitarian form. To the Muslim, God is king and judge. God is transcendent, but not immanent. He cannot conceive how God could take human form and humble himself by suffering on the cross. Therefore he rejects the Incarnation and the love that it reveals.

2. Mutual respect for the Holy Books of both faiths cannot overcome the fact that the Quran disagrees with the Bible at some very crucial points. The most important of these is; "What happened on the cross?" The Muslim prefers to avoid questioning the Quran at this point, for it would threaten his entire theological system to accept the historicity of Jesus' death.

3. The third presupposition proved valid, namely, that **truth about God is accepted by Muslims more readily through the relating of personal experiences than through the use of theological formulae**. Muslims responded freely when I described my own religious experiences. In the case of a Muslim who had accepted Christ, it was discovered that he had done so as a result of a dream which led to a deep mystical experience. He was subsequently open to the truths of the Scriptures.

The achievement of this objective of the project in ministry was evaluated by Dr. Frederick T. Corbin, professor of plant science at N.C.S.U. Dr. Corbin is a former deacon and active member of the Hayes Barton Baptist Church. For a number of years he has served on the B.S.U. Advisory Committee. He had the following evaluation of my relationship with Arab students:

> His ability to speak the Arab language has helped him focus his ministry toward encouraging others to form personal relationships with Muslims. Many Arab students are aware that they have a friend who can understand their concerns,

and who has helped them to make a smooth transition into a foreign land.[5]

The ability to speak Arabic was a definite advantage to me in this phase of the project. Many Arabs were surprised that I was an American because of my fluency in Arabic.

It is only wished that there could have been greater concentration on this phase of ministry to individuals. Six months is a very short time to interact with Muslims and hope to see real progress in their understanding of the Christian Gospel.

The Writer as a Facilitator of Dialogue

Facilitating outreach to Muslim internationals by organizations and individuals was the objective of this phase of the ministry. I served as a resource person on Islam for the Baptist Campus Ministries, the I.V., the Hayes Barton Baptist Church, and various individuals who were associated with Muslims.

As was seen I was able to lead a training session for the B.S.U., but the "Arab Night" program had to be cancelled due to a number of complications. As a result there was no opportunity for Baptist Students to relate to Muslims for dialogue. The M.S.A. banquet was of great value to me for personal dialogue. However, few Baptist students attended. I then became involved in the I.V. international ministry which was found to be highly effective in meeting personal needs of internationals and in presenting the Gospel to them.

Both Mr. Purcell and Mrs. McGee evaluated my work positively as a facilitator of dialogue and resource person on Islam.[6] Dr. Corbin noted, also, my effectiveness in initiating dialogue between Palestinian students and a Sunday School class at Hayes Barton Baptist Church.[7]

An evaluation of the International Student Retreat at Thanksgiving by Mr. Kay Huggins, of North Carolina Campus Ministries, indicated that I had served as a facilitator of dialogue for the Arabian students that attended. These students had responded to me as a bridge of identity with their home culture. This had improved the trust level and contributed to a lessening of their resistance to involvement in group activities.[8]

Another important aspect of this ministry was to train and encourage individuals, who were in contact with Muslims, for more effective dialogue. Miss Luanne Jones, who had been closely related to Iranian students, commented:

> I have been in contact with a large number of Muslims, and being a committed Christian (and known to them as such) it has often been necessary to share in conversation with them about our religions. Knowing and talking with the writer has helped me interact more easily with them. His knowledge of Islam and Middle Eastern culture has helped my understanding and communication with my friends.[9]

Altogether, I worked with ten individuals in the North and South Carolina area to share with them my insights into Islam and to encourage them to carry on a ministry of dialogue with Muslims after I returned to overseas service.

The role of key persons in the university/town complex was vital to me as I attempted to serve as a facilitator of dialogue. These persons, namely Dr. Corbin, Miss Jones, Mr. Huggins, Mrs. McGee, and Mr. Purcell assisted me both in the performance of the project and its subsequent evaluation. One of the most rewarding aspects of this project was my role as a facilitator of dialogue with these key persons.

The Guide to Dialogue Critized, Tested, and Revised

The Guide to Dialogue was used as a training tool and resource for persons engaged in dialogue with Muslims. It was an integral part of the project from beginning to end.

The Guide was shared with twenty persons for evaluation of content, organization, and practicality for use in the Christian-Muslim dialogue. Of the twenty, the writer received fifteen thorough critiques which led to extensive revision. One reviewer was an orthodox Muslim. Another was an Arab Christian. The original draft of thirty-two pages grew to seventy-nine in length. Due to suggestions of reviewers, five of whom were missionaries, sections were added dealing with Arab-Jewish relations and care of new converts. The writer's experiences with Christians married to Muslims led to the inclusion of a section dealing with inter-marriage.

The question-answer approach used in the Guide was found useful by the writer and others. The explanation of the Trinity and the "Son of God" was found to be understandable to both Shi'ite and Sunni Muslims. This explanation removed the offensiveness of the Christian title for Jesus and opened the way to further dialogue.

However, I was never able to receive positive confirmation

of the approach used to explain the cross, or the **shubiha lahum** passage in the Quran. The acceptance of the historicity of Jesus' death on the cross is such a radical step for a Muslim that it undoubtedly would require a longer exposure to Christian teaching than was available in this project. Agreeing with the theological implications of the cross would require an even more radical change of mind for the Muslim. I had found this approach helpful overseas where there was more concentrated exposure to individual Muslims.

Evaluation of the Guide by individuals who were attempting to related to Muslims has been positive with respect to content. The Guide proved invaluable in providing substance to this project. It enabled me to test approaches to Muslims that had been mostly in the realm of speculation in the past.

Limitations of This Ministry in Dialogue

The scope of this project was purposely limited in the beginning to Palestinian Arab Muslims, because of my background and training with that cultural group. There was some difficulty in understanding the dialect of Egyptian and Libyan Arabic in the beginning. The difference in dialect made communication difficult and may have contributed to the confusion in the plans for the "Arab Night" at the B.S.U. As the project proceeded I became more familiar with these dialects and communication became more effective.

In the beginning of the project there was the feeling on my part that my identity with Israel provoked some suspicions of my motives from some Arabs. However, this feeling was totally abolished by the end of the project when Egyptian Arabs began to seek me out at meetings to establish friendships.

Another limitation of the project was the dispersion of Arabs and Muslims throughout the Carolinas. It was not possible to form close friendship with Arabs as far away as Wilmington, North Carolina, or Greenville, South Carolina. Nevertheless, this had the positive effect of requiring me to train persons in those areas and to rely on them for an on-going ministry.

The conflict of theological stances of Christians threatened to limit the effectiveness of dialogue with Muslims. I often felt "caught in the middle" between Christians who evidenced a more open-minded stance toward dialogue and those who felt it was a compromise of their basic convictions. Through this frustration I discovered the necessity of expressing myself more clearly to both sides of the issue. The revised edition of the Guide to Dialogue represents an effort to express my basic Christian convictions more clearly.

One observation became apparent with regard to the theological stance of Christians in the Christian-Muslim dialogue; the direct evangelistic approach employed by some Christians tended to drive Muslims into a strong defense of Islam causing them to become even more devout followers of their faith.

Personal Growth—A Dilemma of Opportunities

Engaging in such a project in the U.S.A. was a radical departure for me, in terms of what I saw as my original calling to the foreign field. It was discovered that in a real sense, the foreign mission field had come home. A degree of inner questioning, especially in the beginning of this project, caused me to ponder the possibility of God's call to minister to Muslims in the U.S.A. on a long-term basis. The question arose of whether the more fruitful field of service could be found at home or abroad. Out of this questioning has come the observation that **there is a basic unity to home and foreign missions, particularly with reference to language missions. Exchange of personnel and utilization of furloughing missionaries should continue as both mission boards seek to minister more effectively to language groups.**

Project as an Assist to Overseas Ministries

Although this project lacked the advantage of total absorption in a Muslim culture, it could provide a model for missionaries and others ministering overseas. The "Guide to Dialogue" will prove useful as it is adapted and revised through field-testing overseas.

Many Muslims contacted during this project will be returning to their home countries to serve in government and education. These may be more favorably disposed toward mission work in their home country as a result of our interchange here. I have been able to contact missions in three cases for follow-up contacts with Muslims who have moved back to the Middle East. In one case a young Muslim is preparing himself to return to his country to share the Gospel with his people.

Discipline of the Project an Asset

The regimen of keeping a diary and writing monthly reports was a definite asset to me. One of the frustrations of overseas service had been the lack of organization in my work as a field evangelist. The clarifying of goals and methodology proved valuable as guidelines for ministry.

Dialogue as an Option to Monologue

In the past I had tended to employ a defensive, monological approach of confrontation with other individuals. The research and performance of this project reinforced my determination to allow the other person to express himself in dialogue. This project has confirmed that a deep confidence in the love of God is a prerequisite to entering into the dialogical role. In this assurance my own ministry has become more effective, not only with Muslims, but with others. **There is great freedom in realizing that God alone is able to interpret truth to the hearts of men through the Holy Spirit. This has relieved me of the burden of producing results that God alone can produce.** This is a saving grace in working with Muslims. The real fruits of this project in dialogue with Muslims may not be realized for years, and others will reap where I have sown.

Opportunities for an On-going Ministry

An opportunity for an on-going ministry of dialogue with Muslims is available in the Raleigh area and in other cities of the Carolinas. This is especially necessary with Muslims because they will not take the initiative to seek out Christian ministries unless some interested person encourages them. The church and its ministries must reach out to them. Baptists and other evangelicals have a unique opportunity to engage in a continuing dialogue because of their historic emphases on religious liberty, Bible-centered piety, and simplicity of worship. The resources of the local churches, conventions, and mission boards should be coordinated to provide for a continuing mission to this language and cultural group. The international population at N.C.S.U. grew 25% in 1976 alone, offering an unprecedented opportunity for similar ministries.

Lay leadership in local churches can continue to perform invaluable service in ministering to Muslims and other internationals. Christian professors at N.C.S.U., as well as college and seminary students, can be encouraged to establish friendships with Muslims.

The Department of Interfaith Witness and Language Missions of the Home Mission Board can reinforce this ministry with seminars on Islam for interested laymen in cities around the country. The assistance of Arab Christian laymen in these areas can be enlisted.

Epilogue

Since the completion of this project the Department of Chaplaincy and Language Ministry of the North Carolina Baptist State Convention has employed a person to minister full-time to Arabs in the state. A survey conducted in 1977 revealed over 20,000 persons of Lebanese origin in North Carolina.

A growing awareness of the opportunity to engage in a ministry of dialogue and interfaith witness to Muslims is developing in this area. Dr. Jackson Rigney, Dean of International Programs at N.C.S.U., summarized the growing interest in the Arab people in a speech before an audience of six-hundred Arabs and Americans at N.C.S.U.:

> We are entering a period of rediscovery of the Arab people . . . We have before us an enormous re-education job to get to know and appreciate the Arab world.[10]

It is hoped that this project will contribute to an on-going dialogue with Muslims that will promote this rediscovery and re-education and lead to peace and understanding between these two great world religions.

Notes to Appendix I

[1]George W. Braswell, Jr., ''Ministry Among Internationals in the Research Triangle Area'' (D. Min. Project Report, Southeastern Baptist Theological Seminary, May 1973.)

[2]Rudolph Malcolm Wood, ''Developing a Continuing Ministry to Internationals'' (D. Min. Project Report, Southeastern Baptist Theological Seminary, April 1974.)

[3]Lonsdale and Laura Ragg, **The Gospel of Barnabas** (Oxford Clarendon Press, 1907.)

[4]Robert E. Coleman, **The Master Plan for Evangelism** (New Jersey: 1973), p. 24.

[5]Appendix 3.

[6]Appendix 3, and Appendix 4.

[7]Appendix 2.

[8]Mr. Kay Huggins, Interview, N.C. Baptist State Convention, January 26, 1976.

[9]Appendix 5.

[10]Dr. Jackson Rigney, Speech, ''Arab Night,'' N.C.S.U., Raleigh, N.C., March 21, 1976.

APPENDIX 2

EVALUATION: TED L. PURCELL

BAPTIST CAMPUS MINISTRY
NORTH CAROLINA STATE UNIVERSITY
P. O. Box 5608 State University Station
Raleigh, North Carolina 27607 — Telephone 834-1875

Ted L. Purcell
Chaplain

March 5, 1976

The following evaluation is offered at the request of Ray Register in relation to his project for the Doctor of Ministry degree at the Southeastern Baptist Theological Seminary. These observations are the result of my having read both the progress reports and the revised write-up of the project **A Guide to Dialogue with Muslims**, and out of my relationship and conversations with Ray Register since the Fall of 1975. I am limited in my competence to evaluate the technical and scholarly dimensions of relating to Muslims and understanding their religion and culture. Therefore, these reflections are directed more to my impressions of Mr. Register as a facilitator of dialogue and to the approaches to Muslims he has employed himself and suggested in the written guide.

I. As a Facilitator of Dialogue

Mr. Register has been helpful as a resource person to Baptist Campus Ministry and the Baptist Student Union at N.C. State University in several ways. On our Fall retreat he spoke briefly and introduced an Arab Christian student who is an officer of the International Student Board at N.C. State. His appearance there served to stimulate interest in a later BSU program on "Relating to Internationals" in which he joined this student and an American student who relates to many international students at N.C. State to offer information and suggestions about building bridges of relationship and sharing one's faith. Later he made me aware of the ministry to internationals which is being sponsored by the Inter-Varsity Christian Fellowship at NCSU, and arranged for a meeting with Mrs. Bette McGee, in whose home the monthly meetings are held. As a follow-up, I received an invitation to visit in these meetings to observe this model of ministry. In addition to other meetings reported in his progress reports, Mr. Register was present for a recent program related to Rev. Moon and the Unification Church, and offered insightful comments during the discussion. I appreciate his sensitivity to the destructive possibilities of certain evangelistic approaches to internationals. I regard him as a person who employs sound principles of communication. He is open, a good listener, seems free of defensiveness, and relates to people at the human level even as he shares the distinctive features of his Christian faith with those whose beliefs are different from his own.

II. The Guide to Dialogue with Muslims

In the process of reading and conversation with Mr. Register I have become aware of numerous aspects of Islam which I had not known, and he has been helpful in enabling me to understand more about the differences and similarities between Muslims and Christians and how these are perceived by members of both religions.

I discover in the guide a concern to relate to Muslims as persons and to form relationships which are the basis for sharing about Christian truth. The Scripture-to-Scripture approach seems to allow for interfaith sharing in a non-argumentative way, and Mr. Register realistically notes that conversion may take place on either side. I appreciate—as one who is interested in the complexities of evangelism in a pluralistic society—that he acknowledges (with Reuel Howe) that "the dialogical role is to take a stand." His guide reflects an awareness of the importance of political situations, customs in male/female relationships, the conflict of ideologies—all of which have a direct bearing on dialogue with Muslims.

III. Opportunities for a similar ministry in the future

I feel that there is a continuing need for dialogue and the sharing of faith and culture with Muslims and other internationals in this geographical area as well as in other places. There is a challenging opportunity here at N.C. State because of the concentration of foreign students and their families.

Perhaps few persons will bring such qualifications as Mr. Register has brought to this task, by virtue of his Christian commitment and experience and expertise. However, it is hoped that others who seek to do this kind of specialized ministry will avail themselves of Mr. Register's written project as well as the doors to relationships which he has opened through his ministry in this area.

Ted L. Purcell
Baptist Campus Minister
N.C. State University

APPENDIX 3

EVALUATION: FREDRICK T. CORBIN

I had the privilege of serving as a member of the North Carolina State University BSU Advisory Committee for seven years and as Chairman of the Advisory Group for two years. Each year one of the major items of concern was the status of our Baptist ministry with international students and their families. The international student ministry was always a challenge to the advisory group. In my opinion, Reverend Ray G. Register, Jr. has been one of the most effective resource persons to serve in the Raleigh area in recent years. Before one can serve effectively as a facilitator of dialogue, one must build bridges of understanding and friendship by crossing religious, racial, cultural, and linguistic barriers. In addition to "building bridges of understanding," Reverend Register has encouraged others to form personal relationships with Muslims. Many Arab students are aware that they have a friend who can understand their concerns, and who has helped to make a smooth transition into a foreign land.

In addition to serving as a resource person, Reverend Register has contributed to our Church fellowship and Sunday School ministry by inviting Palestinian students to share in class meetings. The fellowship established between the Sunday School group and the Palestinian students would have been almost impossible without someone to initiate the dialogue.

The "Guide to Dialogue with Muslims" has contributed to my own life and has increased my understanding of the followers of the religion of Islam. I am more aware that my Muslim friends are persons with similar concerns, feelings, joys, and sorrows, fears and hopes that I have.

Dr. Fredrick T. Corbin
Professor of Plant Science
N.C.S.U.

APPENDIX 4

EVALUATION: LUANNE JONES

1. As a "facilitator of dialogue" with Muslims, the writer has been invaluable to me. I have been in contact with a large number of Muslims, and being a committed Christian (and known to them as such) it has been often necessary to share in conversation with them about our religions. Knowing and talking with the writer has helped me interact much more easily with them. His knowledge of Islam and Middle Eastern culture has helped my understanding and communication with my friends—I have found his advice and knowledge to be very sound and of wide diversity in informativeness.

2. In addition to the statements made in my first answer, may I emphasize the helpfulness of Mr. Register's ministry to my own personal relationships with Muslims. For the past year I have been examining and re-examining each facet of my faith in terms of comparison to Islam. This was a most difficult time for me, and could have been devastating had it not been for Mr. Register's experience and understanding. He helped me to achieve a stability in my own beliefs, which colors every relationship I have with Muslim friends. I can now deal with them from the standpoint of a steady, assured belief.

3. It is difficult for me to separate the writer from the writing in terms of my own knowledge of Islam or dialogue with Muslims, because I was helped so much by the writer before I ever read any of the "Guide." For the average person who has an interest in Islam or who has Muslim friends, the "Guide" should prove most helpful. It is clear and basic, and offers many valuable suggestions for dialogue. The revision has clarified many of the points I questioned on the original.

APPENDIX 5

EVALUATION: MRS. ROBERT D. (Bette) McGEE

We have appreciated Ray Register's help and guidance in the International scene in Raleigh. He has been a valuable resource person in helping us to better understand the Muslim community and in introducing us to Arab students. At our International dinners Ray has had a good rapport with students and made a commendable presentation as speaker for one of our dinners. We have especially appreciated his efforts to enlarge the ministry in this area and to involve others in becoming aware of the needs of foreign students. I have gathered from other students that he has made some in-depth relationships with local Arabs and that they hold him in good regard. I have not had the opportunity to be in a small group with Ray but he has given all indication that he is very well versed and able to present the claims of Christ in a credible way to our Arab friends.

NOTES

INTRODUCTION

1 "Muslim" is the transliteration of an Arabic word. It is sometimes written "Moslem" and you will hear it a variety of ways. "Mohammedan" is an incorrect term and should not be used. "Muhammad" is often written "Mohammed" or "Mohammad."

2 Morroe, Berger, **The Arab World Today** (New York, 1964), p. 234.

Note: Due to fear of persecution by Muslims and political tensions in the Middle East, the Arab Christian is often hesitant to enter into dialogue with Muslims.

3 Reuel L. Howe, **The Miracle of Dialogue** (New York, 1963), pp. 102-103.

CHAPTER I: A BRIEF HISTORY OF ISLAM

1 Muslim population figures are those used at the North American Conference on Muslim Evangelization, Oct. 15-21, 1978 at Colorado Springs.

2 "Allah" is the Arabic word for "God," as distinguished from "ila," "a god." The problem is in the differing understanding of the nature of God in Islam and Christianity.

3 **Shorter Encyclopaedia of Islam**, 1961 ed., s.v. "Bahira."

4 A brief description of the four schools, the Hanifite, the Malikite, the Shafi^{c}ite, and the Hanbalite can be found in **Islam** by Alfred Guillame (Baltimore: 1962), p. 102.

5 See Guillaume, **Islam**, pp. 115-125, and George W. Braswell, Jr., **To Ride a Majic Carpet** (Nashville, 1977), for a more thorough description of Shi'ite beliefs.

CHAPTER II: DIALOGUE AS A METHOD OF APPROACH TO MUSLIMS

1 Reuel L. Howe, **The Miracle of Dialogue,** (New York, 1963), p. 4.

2 Ibid., pp. 5-7

3 Ibid., pp. 151-152

4 Rt. Rev. Hassan Barnabus Dehqani-Tafti, Anglican Bishop of Iran, "My View of Christian Missions among Muslims," "Teheran Conference," Report, June 22-27, 1969, Southern Baptist Missions in the Middle East, p. 3.

5 The Rev. Paul Seto, "Personal Reflections on Muslim-Christian Relations," "Teheran Conference," p. 7.

6 Kenneth Cragg, **The Call of the Minaret** (New York, 1964), p. 245.

7 Rev. Iradj Mottahedeh, "Critical Problems and Creative Opportunities," "Teheran Conference," p. 4.

8 Howe, **Miracle of Dialogue**, p. 103.

9 Dehqani-Tafti, "Teheran Conference," p. 8.

10 Kate Ellen Gruver, Interview, Atlanta, Ga., October 3, 1975.

11 W. Montgomery Watt, **Islamic Revelation in the Modern World** (Edinburgh, 1969), p. 125.

12 I am indebted in this section to Dr. Elmer H. Douglas for class notes on "The Christian Mission to Islam," 1964, and to Dr. R. Marston Speight for class notes on "Islam and the West," 1970, taught at the Hartford Seminary Foundation, Hartford, Connecticut.

13 Nicholas Rescher, "Nicholas of Cusa on the Qur'an," **M.W.**, 3, 1965, p. 195.

14 Rev. Ignatius C. Brady, "Saint Francis," **Encyclopaedia Britannica,** 1973 ed., Vol. 9, p. 708b.

15 Robert Duqid Forrest Pring-Mill, "Ramon Lull," **Encyclopaedia Britannica,** 1973 ed., Vol. 14, p. 173b.

16 Rescher, op. cit., p. 196.

17 F. Julius Basetti-Sani, "Dialogue Between Christians and Muslims," **M.W.**, 2, 1967, p. 128.

18 William Whitfield Stennett, "The Christian Missionary Confronts the Muslim," (Th.M. Thesis, S.E.B.T.S., April, 1959), p. 35.

19 Cragg, **Call of the Minaret,** Chapters vii-xi.

20 Bassetti-Sani, op. cit., p. 126.

21 **M.W.**, 1, 1975, pp. 67-69. 22 **M.W.**, 2, 1975, pp. 132-36.

23 **M.W.**, 3, 1975, pp. 233-34.

24 **Bilalian News**, March 5, 1976, p. 1.

25 **Christians Meeting Muslims,** W.C.C. Papers on 10 Years of Christian Muslim Dialogue (Geneva, 1977).

26 Howe, **Miracle of Dialogue**, pp. 21-31.

27 Charles Austin Beckett, "Sin and Salvation in Islam," (Th.M. Thesis, S.E.B.T.S., April 1958), p. 27.

28 Ibid., p. 32. 29 Ibid., p. 36. 30 Ibid., p. 44.

31 Morroe Berger, **The Arab World Today** (New York, 1964), p. 139.

32 C. George Fry, "Christianity's Greatest Challenge," (F.F.M., reprint from **Christianity Today**, 1969), pp. 4-6.

33 Daud Rahbar, **God of Justice**, (Leiden, 1960), pp. 224-5).

34 Akbar Abdul-Haqq, **Christ in the New Testament and the Quran** (Taken from a Ph.D. Dissertation at Northwestern University, June 1973), p. 17.

35 Ibid., p. 23.

36 Charles Malik, **God and Man in Contemporary Islamic Thought** (Beirut, 1972), pp. 91-92.

37 Johni Johnson, **The Gift of Belonging** (Nashville, 1975), pp. 147-149, 152.

Chapter III: GENERAL GUIDELINES TO DIALOGUE WITH MUSLIMS

1 W. St. Clair-Tisdall, **The Sources of Islam**, Trans. by William Muir (England, n.d.), pp. 56-58.

2 The average Muslim believes that Muhammad received his revelations directly from God and that he was not dependant upon any human source for inspiration.

3 The Ahmadiyya sect of Islam believes Jesus was crucified, but only swooned on the cross. He was revived by a mysterious ointment in the tomb,

arose and went to Kashmir, India, where he died at the age of 120. The Ahmadiyya sect is considered heretical by orthodox Islam. It has active mission work among Muslims and Christians.

4 **Shorter Encyclopedia of Islam**, 1961 ed., s.v. "khati'a."

5 Romans 3:23-24, I Timothy 2:5-6, Ephesians 2:8-9.

6 The disagreement here is not with "soul-winning" or the "plan of salvation." These are valid approaches and biblically sound when used with persons who are ready to accept them. But the Muslim is usually not at the place where these approaches have any meaning. Preparation or "pre-evangelism" is necessary.

7 The Navigators have written and tested a "Scripture to Scripture" approach to sin and salvation using both the Bible and the Quran entitled, "Have You Ever Read the Seven Muslim Christian Principles," available from Ar-Rabitah, P.O. Box 1433, Limassol, Cyprus.

8 **Your Muslim Guest** (F.F.M.), will be very helpful in understanding some of the social customs of Muslims.

CHAPTER IV: QUESTIONS AND STATEMENTS ENCOUNTERED IN DIALOGUE WITH MUSLIMS

1 H. A. L. Fisher, **A History of Europe** (Boston, 1936), p. 148. Quoted from Stennet, op. cit., p. 19.

2 A. Yusif Ali, **The Holy Quran**, note 4783 and 4784, p. 1368.

3 **Interlinear Greek-English New Testament**, by George Ricker Berry, (Grand Rapids, 1958-75).

4 Ali, **The Holy Quran**, note 5438, p. 1540.

5 Ibid. 6. See B. 4.

7 W. Montgomery Watt, **Islamic Revelation in the Modern World** (Edinburgh, 1969), p. 20.

8 Gleason Archer, **A Survey of the Old Testament** (Chicago, 1964), p. 19. Quoted from Josh McDowell, **Evidence that Demands a Verdict** (San Bernidino, Campus Crusade for Christ, 1972), p. 61.

9 **The Interpreter's Bible**, 1951 ed., Sherman E. Johnson, "Text," Vol. 7, p. 244.

10 Burton H. Throckmorton, Jr., **Gospel Parallels** (New York, 1957), vi.

11 Surahs II:59, 75, III:78, IV:46, V:13, 41, VII:17.

12 Ali, **The Holy Quran**, Appendix III, p. 287. Note: This view of the Bible may not be accepted by more conservative Muslims.

13 Lonsdale and Laura Ragg, **The Gospel of Barnabas** (Oxford, 1907), republished by Begum Aisha Bawany Wakf, Karachi, Pakistan, 1973).

14 John Lawson, **The Biblical Theology of Saint Irenaeus** (London, 1948), p. 250.

15 James Cannon, III, "The Gospel of Barnabas," **M.W.**, Vol. 32, 1942, pp. 167-178. Also Selim 'Abdul-Ahad, and W.H.T. Gairdner, **The Gospel of Barnabas** (F.F.M.), p. 13ff.

16 The number of the section in the **Gospel of Barnabas** is listed after each reference.

17 'Abdul-Ahad and Gairdner, op.cit., p. 11 refer to an Italian monk, Fra Marino, who claimed to have discovered the original manuscript with Pope Sixtus V (A.D. 1585-1589) and converted to Islam.

18 A helpful book for this approach is by I. Bevan Jones, **Christianity Explained to Muslims**, Revised Edition, 1964, available from F.F.M.

19 Joseph M. Raya, **The Face of God** (Denville, N.J., 1976), p. 120 ff.

20 **The Interpreter's One-Volume Commentary**, e.v., Hebrews 1-2, p. 899.

21 C. R. Marsh, **Share Your Faith With a Muslim** (Chicago, 1975), Chapter 8, gives an excellent presentation on the uniqueness of Christ.

22 M. R. James, **The Apocryphal New Testament** (Oxford, 1926), p. 254.

23 Henry M. Shires, **Finding the Old Testament in the New** (Philadelphia, 1974), p. 104.

24 Books that will acquaint you with the intensity of the Arab hostility in the Palestinian issue and the release that can come through faith in Christ are: James & Marti Hefly, **The Liberated Palestinian,** The Anis Shurrosh Story (Wheaton, 1975) and **Arabs, Christians and Jews** (Plainfield, N.J., 1978).

CHAPTER VI: WHAT TO DO FOR PERSONS WHO DECIDE TO CHANGE THEIR FAITH

1 Phil Parshall, "Evangelizing Muslims: Are There Ways?" **Christianity Today**, January 5, 1979, pp. 28 ff.

ABBREVIATIONS

F.F.M.	Fellowship of Faith for Muslims
I.R.M.	International Review of Missions
M.W.	Muslim World Quarterly
S.E.B.T.S.	Southeastern Baptist Theological Seminary
W.C.C.	World Council of Churches

BIBLIOGRAPHY
AND
RECOMMENDED READING

The following sources are recommended for background for the Christian-Muslim dialogue and interfaith witness with Muslims.

Abd al-Fadi, **The Person of Christ in the Gospel and Quran**, Translated, Center for Young Adults, Basil, n.d.

'Abdul-Ahad, Selim, and Gairdner, W.H.T., **The Gospel of Barnabas, An Essay and Inquiry**, Hyderbad, 1975 (F.F.M.)

Abdul-Haqq, Dr. Akbar, **Christ in the New Testament and Quran,** 3628 Orchard Ave. N., Minneapolis, Minnesota 55422, 1975.

Accad, Fuad, "The Qur'an A Bridge to Christian Faith," **Missiology**, 3 (1976), 331-342.

Addison, James Thayer, **The Christian Approach to Muslims**, New York, 1942.

Alavi, K. K., **In Search of Assurance**, Bombay, 1977.

Ali, A. Yusif, **The Holy Qur'an**, Text, Translation, Commentary, Washington, D.C., 1964.

Anderson, John D.C., "The Missionary Approach to Islam: Christian or Cultic?", **Missiology**, 3 (1976), 285-300.

Andrae, Tor, **Mohammed, the Man and His Faith**, New York, 1960.

Arberry, A. J., **The Koran Interpreted**, New York, 1955-1974.

Bavinck, J. H., **The Church Between Temple and Mosque**, Michigan, n.d.

Barclay, Harold B., "The Perpetuation of Muslim Tradition in the Canadian North," **M.W.**, 1 (1969), 64.

Basetti-Sani, F. Julius, "For a Dialogue Between Christians and Muslims (1)," **M.W.**, 2 (1967), 126-137.

Beckett, Charles Austin, "Sin and Salvation in Islam," Th.M. Thesis, S.E.B.T.S., 1958.

Bell, R., **The Origin of Islam in Its Christian Environment,** London, 1926.

Berger, Morroe, **The Arab World Today**, New York, 1964.

Bethman Erich, **Bridge to Islam**, London, 1953.

________, **Steps Toward Understanding Islam**, Washington, D.C., 1966.

Bevan Jones, L., "Our Message to Muslims," **M.W.**, 20 (1930), 331-336.

________, **Christianity Explained to Muslims,** Calcutta, 1952.

________, **From Islam to Christ**—Life of Bishop J. Subhan, Focus on Islam Series, F.F.M., n.d.

Bijlefeld, Willem A., "Recent Theological Evaluation of the Christian-Muslim Encounter (Part II)," **I.R.M.**, 55 (1966), 430-441.

Braswell, George W. Jr., "Ministry Among Internationals in the Research Triangle Area," D. Min. Project Report. S.E.B.T.S., 1973.

________, **To Ride a Majic Carpet**, Nashville, 1977.

Browne, Laurence, E., **The Quickening Word: A Theological Answer to the**

Challenge of Islam, (Hulsean Lectures, 1954), Cambridge, 1955.
Brown, David, **Christianity and Islam Series,** London, 1967ff.
Budd, Jack, **Studies on Islam,** A Simple Outline of the Islamic Faith, Red Sea Team, n.d. (F.F.M.)
Cash, W. W., **Christendom and Islam: Their Contacts and Cultures Down the Centuries,** London, 1937.
Christian Witness Among Muslims: A Handbook for Christians of Africa (South of Sahara), Accra, Ghana, 1971-1977.
Christiansen, Jens, **The Practical Approach to Muslims,** Mardan, Pakistan, 1952-1953.
Coleman, Robert E., **The Master Plan of Evangelism**, New Jersey, 1973.
Conference of European Churches and European Liason Committee of the Islam in Africa Project, **The Church and the Muslim in Europe—Matters for Reflection,** Report of a Consultation held in Salzburg, Austria 6-11 February, 1978, Geneva, 1978.
Cragg, A. Kenneth, "Each Other's Face: Some Thoughts on Muslim-Christian Colloquy Today," **M.W.**, 45 (1955), 172-182.
________, **The Call of the Minaret**, New York, 1956.
________, **Sandals in the Mosque, Christian Presence Amid Islam,** New York, 1959.
________, "Introduction" to **City of Wrong, A Friday in Jerusalem,** by Kamel Hussein, London, 1959.
________, **Christianity in World Perspective,** New York, 1968.
________, **The Event of the "Qur'an,** Winchester, MA, 1978.
Cutler, Allen, "The Ninth-Century Spanish Martyrs' Movement, and the Origins of Western Christian Missions to the Muslims," **M.W.**, 4 (1965), 321-339.
________, "The First Crusade and the Idea of 'Conversion'," **M.W.**, 2 (1968), 155-164.
Dehquani-Tafti, Hassan, **Design of My World**, London, 1959.
Devannadan, P. D., **Preparation for Dialogue**, Bangalore, 1964.
Elder, J., **Biblical Approach to the Muslim**, Hong Kong, n.d. (F.F.M.)
Encyclopedia of Islam, The (Editors, M. T. Houtsma, T. W. Arnold, et al.) 4 Vols., Leiden, 1913-36; new edition, Vol. I-., Leiden, 1960-.
de Epalza, Mikel, "Cordova Welcomes its Muslim Friends," **M.W.**, 2, (1975), 132-136.
Foster, F. H., "Is Islam a Christian Heresy?" **M.W.**, 22 (1932), 126-133.
Fry, C. George, "Christianity's Greatest Challenge," F.F.M., Toronto (Reprint from **Christianity Today**, 1969).
Franks, Robert S., **The Doctrine of the Trinity,** Duckworths Theological Series, London, 1953.
The Gospel and Islam, A 1978 Compendium, ed. Don McCurry, MARC, Monrovia, CA, 1979.
Gibb, H.A.R., **Mohommedanism: An Historical Survey**, London (2nd ed.), 1953.
________, and Kramers, J. H., **Shorter Encyclopaedia of Islam,** New York, 1961.
The Glen Eyrie Report, A Lausanne Occasional Paper, MARC, 1979.
Goldsmith, Martin, "Community and Controversy: Key Causes of Muslim Resistance," **Missiology**, 3 (1976), 317-324.
Gruver, Kate Ellen, "Muslims on the American Scene," **Home Missions,** Atlanta, March 1975, 38-43.

Guillaume, Alfred, **Islam**, Baltimore, 1962.
Hanna, Mark, **The True Path, Seven Muslims Make Their Greatest Discovery**, Colorado Springs, 1975.
Hargreaves, A. R., "A Method of Presenting Jesus Christ to Moslems," **M.W.**, 37 (1947), 255-265.
Harris, G. K., **How to Lead Moslems to Christ**, Philadelphia, 1947.
Harrison, Anne M., **A Tool in His Hand,** New York, 1958.
Have You Ever Read the Seven Muslim Christian Principles, Ar-Rabitah, POB 1433, Limassol, Cyprus, 1978.
Hefley, James and Marti, **The Liberated Palestinian,** Wheaton, 1975.
________, **Arabs, Christians, Jews,** Plainfield, N.J., 1978.
Hitti, Philip K., **History of the Arabs,** New York, 1964.
________, **History of Seria,** London, 1951.
________, **The Arabs: A Short History,** Princeton, 1970.
________, **Islam, A Way of Life,** Chicago, 1970.
Howe, Reuel, L., **The Miracle of Dialogue,** New York, 1963.
Jadeed, Iskander, **The Cross in the Gospel and the Quran,** Translated, Center for Young Adults, Basel, n.d.
James, M. R., **The Apocryphal New Testament,** Oxford, 1926.
Jeffery, Arthur, "The Presentation of Christianity to Moslems," **I.R.M.,** 13 (1924), 174-189.
Johnson, Johni, **The Gift of Belonging,** The Story of Virginia Cobb, Missionary to Muslims, Nashville, 1975.
Jones, L. Bevan, **Christianity Explained to Muslims,** Revised Edition, Calcutta, 1964. (F.F.M.)
Kerr, David, "Personal Encounters with Muslims and Their Faith," **Missiology,** 3 (1976), 325-330.
Kershaw, Max, **How to Share the Good News with Your Muslim Friend,** Colorado Springs, 1978.
Khair-Ullah, F. S., "Evangelism Among Muslims," **Let the Earth Hear His Voice,** Minneapolis, 1975. 816ff.
________, "Linguistic Hang-ups in Communicating with Muslims," **Missiology,** 3 (1976), 301-316.
Khan, Muhammad Zafrulla, **The Quran,** Arabic Text, English Translation, London, 1971.
Kirk, George, **A Short History of the Middle East, from the Rise of Islam to Modern Times,** London, 1948.
Kraemer, Hendrik, "Syncretism as a Religious and a Missionary Problem," **I.R.M.,** 43 (1954), 253-273.
________, **World Culture and World Religions: The Coming Dialogue,** Philadelphia, 1960.
Lewis, Benard, **The Arabs in History,** London, 1958.
Little, Paul E., **A Guide to International Friendship,** I.V.C.F., 1971.
________, **How to Give Away Your Faith,** Downers Grove, Ill., 1975.
Lovell, Emily Kalled, "A Survey of the Arab-Muslims in the United States and Canada," **M.W.,** 2 (1973), 139ff.
Macdonald, Duncan Black, **Development of Muslim Theology Jurisprudence and Constitutional Theory,** London, 1903.
Malik, Charles, **God and Man in Contemporary Islamic Thought,** Beirut, 1960.
Margoliouth, D. S., "Islam a Christian Heresy?" **M.W.,** 23 (1933), 6-15.
Marsh, C. R., **Too Hard For God?,** Bath, 1970.

________, **Share Your Faith With a Muslim,** Chicago, 1975.
McCurry, Don M., "Cross-Cultural Models for Muslim Evangelism," **Missiology,** 3 (1976), 267-284.
Merril, J. E., "A Christian 'Word of Testimony' of Use with Muslims," **Macdonald Presentation Volume,** Princeton, 1933, 193ff.
Miller, William McElvee, **A Christian Response to Islam,** Philadelphia, 1976.
________, **Ten Muslims Meet Christ,** Grand Rapids, 1969.
Neilsen, Alfred, **William Temple Gairdner,** Copenhage, 1932.
________, "Difficulties in Presenting the Gospel," **M.W.,** 19 (1929), 41-46.
Nolin, Kenneth E., "al-Masih fi 'l-Qur'an wa 'l-Tawrat wa 'l-Injil, Book Review, **M.W.,** 1 (1969), 74-79.
________, "Christ in the Qur'an, the Taurat, and the Injil," by 'Abd al-Karim al-Khatib, translated and annotated, **M.W.,** 2 (1971), 90-101.
Noss, John B., "Islam: The Religion of Submission to God in Interaction with Various Cultures," **Man's Religions,** New York, 1974, 507-557.
Odunaike, Samuel, "Cracks in the Muslim Wall," **Church Growth Bulletin,** 2 (1978), Santa Clara, CA.
Padwick, C., **Henry Martyn, Confessor of the Faith,** New York, 1923.
________, **Temple Gairdner of Cairo,** London, 1929.
Parrinder, Geoffrey, **Jesus in the Quran,** London, 1965.
Parshall, Phil, "Evangelizing Muslims: Are There Ways?" **Christianity Today,** January 5, 1979, 28ff.
Picthall, Marmaduke, **The Meaning of the Glorious Koran,** New York, 1954.
Pfander, Karl G., **Mizan-ul-Haqq** (Balance of Truth), London, 1910.
Radley, Miss C., **The Muslim Challenge to the Christian Church,** Focus on Islam Series, F.F.M., n.d.
Ragg, Lonsdale and Laura, **The Gospel of Barnabus,** Oxford, 1907.
Rahbar, Daud, **God of Justice,** Leiden, 1960.
________, "Christian Apologetic to Muslims," **I.R.M.,** 54 (1965) 353-359.
Raya, Joseph M., Archbishop, **The Face of God: An Introduction to Eastern Spirituality,** New Jersey, 1976.
Rescher, Nicholas, "Nicholas of Cusa on the Qur'an," **M.W.,** 3 (1965), 195ff.
Reports of Conferences on Muslim-Christian Dialogue, Hong Kong, Jan. 4-10, 1975, Muslims and Christians in Society, Towards Good-will, Consultation and Working Together in Southeast Asia," **M.W.,** 3 (1975), 233-234.
________, Ghana, Spain and Tunisia, 1974, **M.W.,** 3 (1975), 67-69. "Islamic Christian Dialogue," Seminar Feb. 1976, Tripoli, UN Libyan Mission, New York, n.d.
Speight, R. Marston, "Some Bases for a Christian Apologetic to Islam," **I.R.M.,** 54 (1965), 193-205.
Stacey, Vivienne, "Toward a Current Strategy: Discerning God's Hand in Islam Today," **Missiology,** 3 (1976), 363-372.
Stennett, W. W., "The Christian Missionary Confronts the Moslem," Th.M. Thesis, S.E.B.T.S., 1959.
"Teheran Conference, 1969," Report of Southern Baptist Missions in the Middle East (Mimeographed).
Tisdall, W. St. Clair, **The Sources of Islam,** (Trans. Wm. Muir), Edinburgh, 1901.
Trimingham, J. S., **Christianity Among the Arabs in Pre-Islamic Times,** Leiden, 1978.
Vander, Werff, Lyle L., **Christian Mission to Muslims,** Pasadena, 1977.

Von Sicard, S., "Contemporary Islam and Its World Mission," **Missiology**, 3 (1976), 343-362.
Waardenburg, Dr. Jacobus, "Massignon: Notes for Further Research," **M.W.**, 3 (1966), 157-172.
Waltz, James, "Historical Perspectives on 'Early Missions' to Muslims. A Response to Allan Cutler," **M.W.**, 3 (1971), 170-186.
Watt, W. Montgomery, **What is Islam?** Arabic Background Series, London, 1968.
———, **Islamic Revelation in the Modern World**, Edinburgh, 1969.
———, "Thoughts on Muslim-Christian Dialogue," **M.W.**, 1 (1967), 19-23.
Wilson, J. Christy, **Introducing Islam**, New York, 1965.
Wood, Rudolph Malcolm, "Developing a Continuing Ministry to Internationals," D.Min. Project Report, S.E.B.T.S., 1974.
World Council of Churches;

New Approaches to Men of other Faiths: a Theological Discussion, 1938-1968, Geneva, 1970.

Dialogue Between Men of Living Faiths, Ajaltoun Consultation, Lebanon, March 1970, Ed. S. J. Samartha, Geneva, 1971.

Living Faith and the Ecumenical Movement, Ed. S. J. Samartha, Geneva, 1971.

Christian-Muslim Dialogue, Papers from Broumana, 1972, Eds. S. J. Samartha and J. B. Taylor, Geneva, 1973.

Living Faiths and Ultimate Goals, Ed. S. J. Samartha, Geneva, 1974.

Memoranda: Muslim-Christian Dialogues, Legon, Ghana, July 1974: The Unity of God and the Community of Mankind, Hong Kong, January, 1975.

Christians Meeting Muslims: WCC Papers on 10 Years of Christian-Muslim Dialogue, Geneva, 1977.

Your Muslim Guest, A Practical Guide in Friendship and Witness for Christians Who Meet Muslims in North America, Toronto, F.F.M., n.d.

Many of these sources and other helpful information can be obtained from:

Fellowship of Faith for Muslims
205 Yonge Street, Room 25
Toronto, Ontario, Canada
M5B IN2